Gnome

A FOREWORD FROM LORD GNOME
CHAIRMAN GNOME INTERNATIONAL PLC
PROPRIETOR DAILY GNOME

I WAS both delighted and honoured when it was suggested that I should write a foreword to this publication. I was doubly flattered when it became clear that the suggestion had come from a distinguished figure in the publishing world and one who has close links with charitable work throughout the country ie myself.

Firstly I would like to make it clear that I have from the very beginning been an admirer and supporter of Mr Geldof. Reports that I described him on one occasion as "a jumped up bog trotting hippy who needs a good horse whipping" are completely untrue and in any case have been quoted out of context. The exact context escapes me at the moment but I believe what I said at the time was that it was tremendously exciting to see young people "jumping up and down, trotting about happily and having a whip round for a good cause".

Since my initial support for Live Aid my admiration for Mr Geldof has increased and my own organ, The Daily Gnome, has run a vociferous campaign in support of his elevation to the Peerage. The recent editorial "Gor Blimey Let's have Lord Bob for crying out loud!" put his case particularly well. Again there were unfounded reports that I had earlier objected to having "a thick Banjo Player" in the Upper House. Nothing could be further from the truth. Whilst the traditions of the House of Lords are best maintained by the long established families like that of Gnome (first Duke of Neasden 1961) there can be no objection to more colourful characters like Lord Robert of Boomtown being admitted from time to time. Whether the title should extend to the Hon Fifi Trixibelle is a matter for debate but it is no time surely for pettiness.

The achievements of Band Aid, Live Aid and Sport Aid are not to be dismissed lightly, despite the influential voices that have been raised in criticism. One thinks particularly of the popular radio personality Sid Yobbo and the even more popular television personality Jonathan King. However I shall not be joining them, not even after the disappointment of my own Gnome Aid which raised saddeningly small amounts of money for a charity rather nearer home (The Distressed Aristocrats in the Upper Tax Brackets Fund). Still, giving money is not everything. For that reason I am not going to give any money to Comic Relief. I feel that in this case my best wishes will mean so much more. I shall of course think of your work on my forthcoming fact-finding tour of the distressed continent that is in all our thoughts.

Best Wishes,
E. Strobes
pp. Lord Gnome
The Penthouse Suite
The Golden Nugget Hotel
Sun City
Yesbwanaland
South Africa.

THE UTTERLY UTTERLY MERRY COMIC RELIEF CHRISTMAS BOOK CONTENTS

Preface
A Christmas Message
From The Cabinet Secretary
Sir Humphrey Appleby

10 DOWNING STREET
WHITEHALL SW1A 2AB

I beg to crave the momentary indulgence of the Reader in order to discharge a by no means disagreeable obligation which has over the years become more or less established practice, within the government circles in which we move, as we approach the terminal period of the year – calendar, of course not financial – in fact, not to put too fine a point on it, week fifty-one of the year – and I should like to submit to the Reader with all appropriate deference, for his consideration at a convenient juncture, a sincere and sanguine expectation, indeed confidence, indeed one might even go so far as to say <u>hope</u> that the aforementioned period may, at the end of the day, when all relevant factors have been taken into consideration, be susceptible of being deemed to be such as to merit a verdict of having been by no means unsatisfactory in its overall outcome and, in the final anlysis, to give grounds for being judged, on mature reflection, to have been conducive to generating a degree of gratification, relaxation and celebration which will be seen in retrospect to have been significantly higher than the general average.

Sir Humphrey Appleby, KCB, MVO, MA (Oxon

The Night Before Christmas –
Neighbourhood Watch Version

'Twas the night before Christmas
When all through the house
Not a creature was stirring
Not even a mouse.
The stockings were hung
From the chimney with care
In hope that St Nicholas
Soon would be there.
And Ma in her nightgown
And me in my cap
Had just settled down
For a long winter's nap
When up on the roof
there arose such a clatter
That I got out of bed
To see what was the matter

But first I reached out
For the gun by my bed
To pump the intruder
Gut full of lead.
I crept out the door
And on to the lawn
Those housebreaking bastards
Had seen their last dawn.
Out in the moonlight
Seven shadows I saw.
There was no time for thinking —
I dropped to the floor.
Bang bang bang bang
Bang bang and bang
Through the still winter's night
My bold twelve bore sang.
Down from the roof
Fell the seven dead crooks.
I crossed over the drive
To take a good look.
Six reindeer it was,
And a fat guy in red.
A strange bunch of villains,
But now they were dead.
So I went back to bed
Full of Christmas good cheer.
I'd helped keep our neighbourhood
Kids free from fear.

'ello Readers,

It is my pleasure to introduce to you, a great little page - probably one of the most interesting pages around for some time. Not your average any old page, but page forty-eight! (48)

There is a slight problem however. It appears to be a _very_ popular page and we have found it has a squatter on it! Michael something or other, but we can assure you we are dealing with him, and will have him removed A.S.A.P.

Yours truly,

George Harrison M.B.E.

Biggles
AND THE GROUPIES
BY MICHAEL PALIN
ILLUSTRATIONS BY GLEN BAXTER

BIGGLES – AS OTHERS SAW HIM

Major James Bigglesworth, or Biggles as we all know him, was a curiously enigmatic figure. We know he smoked, and ejaculated frequently (though not as frequently as Algy). He also smiled grimly, replied curtly, observed reflectively and occasionally felt a sudden sense of disappointment. But what of those who really *knew him? What of the private Biggles? The man behind the flying mask? Recently several people who knew Biggles intimately for a few hours have been persuaded to go into print by the hugely successful English Sunday newspaper the Arsehole of the World.*

Comic Relief has secured the exclusive pre-publication world rights to the revelations which have rocked the literary and aeronautical world to its foundations. Not since it was revealed that Beatrix Potter was on smack and that Ernest Hemingway cried when he read Rupert has there been such a shattering reappraisal. Comic Relief Books (Panama and Grand Cayman Inc.) Ltd proudly presents:

BIGGLES AND THE GROUPIES

Sandra X was just eighteen when she met the air ace at a party in Copenhagen . . .

"There was something about him as soon as he entered the room . . . he looked very lost, vulnerable almost. He was entirely dressed in leather and quite a few heads turned. I was with Archie Rice-Buggershaw, the mint lump magnate, who was boring me dreadfully with his ostrich stories, so I slipped away under pretext of going for a shit and soon found myself close to the attractive, enigmatic newcomer. He looked at me. I looked at him and the chemistry began to work. He turned light green and I gave off a faintly acrid ammonic smell.

He offered me a cigarette. I could tell from his tanned index finger that he was no stranger to the Craven 'A's.

"D'you fancy something a bit stronger . . ." I asked.

"Like Passing Clouds?" he returned evenly. I didn't know what he was talking about but that didn't matter. Those three words were the most beautiful I'd ever heard in the English language.

I knew I was hopelessly, helplessly in love with this man.

He must have sensed my confusion for he told me that he'd just been in the Baltic. Before that he'd been South, North, East and West and had also Seen It Through.

Somehow, we found ourselves in the kitchen together. There were only two other people there – "Snarler" Rubinstein and Betty "The Back" Bumstead. As they heaved and rogered away, occasionally breaking off to readjust their position or close the door of the fridge, we chattered on about all sorts of trivial things – the length of an elephant's penis, cures for rubella, why Ely Cathedral wasn't built upside down – anything, but what I really wanted to know – did he care for me enough to have my child, or at least try to? We ate a bit of cheese. By now "Snarler" and "The Back" were approaching orgasm so we made a polite excuse and left.

We found ourselves on the balcony. Outside, the huge ferris-wheel in the Tivoli gardens

ARCHIE RICE-BUGGERSHAW WAS BORING
ME DREADFULLY WITH HIS OSTRICH STORIES...

Biggles

AND THE GROUPIES

BY MICHAEL PALIN
ILLUSTRATIONS BY GLEN BAXTER

rose and fell and below us the night scents of Copenhagen rose pungently to our nostrils. I didn't feel we had to say anything at all. I just felt incredibly safe and secure.

He asked me whether I'd ever smoked Three Castles. I said no. He said he would get some for me when he was next back in England. He talked a lot about tobacconists, how they ran their businesses and how they had helped him over hard times in his life. He asked me what I did. I told him I was a prostitute. He said prostitutes smoked a lot. I told him this was only in films and that nowadays a lot of prostitutes were health freaks.

I noticed a trace of anger cross his face – the first disagreeable emotion I'd noticed all evening. "This damn link between smoking and ill-health," he muttered. "It's never been satisfactorily proven." I asked him about the tests on rats, but this just made him even angrier. "What do rats know about smoking?" he almost shouted . . . "Should a great company like du Maurier be ruined on the word of a rat!"

By this time I was getting a little out of my depth and anxious for a little nookie and some hot chocolate. I touched his arm, but he pulled away . . . "There is no conclusive evidence to link deaths from cancer and smoking . . ."

"It's a major contributory factor, surely," I said.

"No . . . no . . . no! . . . It can't be!" he shouted, and I noticed that his cheeks were wet with tears.

I'm old enough to know when a man wants to be alone, so I stepped indoors, trod on some fish pâté and never saw him again.

It was only several years later when I was tossing off Tiny, now Sir Tiny, Bulstrode that I learnt who my mysterious companion of the night had been. And what's more, the very next morning he'd quit smoking.

Everyone has stories of Biggles's legendary sexual prowess, but none as unusual as that of "Baby" Wattles, an American shoe-tree millionairess who met Bigglesworth at one of D. H. Lawrence's literary evenings . . . She remembers . . .

"Biggles was an absolute sweetie. The only man I know who smoked before, after and during intercourse. He was wonderfully gallant in a very old-fashioned way and when I was stuck in charades he would always whisper little clues. D. H. Lawrence had been a chicken for ages and was getting very red-faced and angry when Biggles nudged me and muttered "Plumed Serpent." I came straight out with it and Lawrence was terribly relieved. Then we made love and listened to the news. Biggles was obsessed by the fear that a world war might break out without his knowing, and took a radio with him everywhere. And this was before the days of portable radios. Wires trailed all over the place and once when he took me to lunch at the Connaught he was sent up the tradesmen's stairs."

"Gang Bangs" involving Biggles and his two chums Algy and Ginger were said to have taken place at a house in Reigate, but there is little hard evidence. Miss Windward Isles 1927 says she remembers an erotic night with the three fliers . . .

HE TOOK A RADIO WITH HIM EVERYWHERE...

"They were fed up with being thought of as homosexuals, and rang me up and asked me to come down to a camshaft repair shop near Weybridge to pick up some parts. There was a lot of giggling as they said this, and I thought it was schoolboys doing Geography 'O' level again – I'm in the phone book under Windward Isles, you see. But suddenly a different voice came on. He sounded very authoritative and apologised for his friends. He said he had only a couple of hours to live and could I come round to see him without much on.

He gave me an address in Hertfordshire, and being one for a bit of an adventure – Windward Isles by name, Windward Isles by nature! – I decided to give it a try.

Well, 117 Woodside Lane turned out to be an airfield. I walked for about half a mile up one of the runways, feeling a bit of a fool, but at last I saw a crack of light in one of the hangars and there, silhouetted against the light, stood a man with the biggest stiffy I'd ever seen (and believe me there are some big ones in the Windward Isles). Honestly it was an Eyeful Tower, a Nelson's Column of a nudger and I'm afraid I just screamed with delight and shone my torch at it. What a disappointment, it was a camshaft after all. The boy who was holding it had nice ginger hair though and soon we were nibbling canapés and sipping a Baltic wine that Biggles had brought back from one of his stories.

Ginger introduced me to his friend Algy, who also had a big camshaft. He said they'd been re-bored and they were greasing them ready for installation.

Ginger and Algy giggled together a lot and

N° 117 WOODSIDE LANE TURNED OUT
TO BE AN AIRFIELD...

when Biggles asked me if I wanted to see in the cockpit, they nearly split their sides. I felt very sorry for Biggles because he clearly wanted a going-over but didn't know how to ask. Then I noticed something about Ginger and his friend. The more they rubbed their camshafts the happier they seemed to be. Being a lifelong cricket fan I know quite a lot about mind-bending substances so I went over to one of the camshafts and had a sniff. It was sensational. I grabbed the tin of "Wilkinson's Number 12 Industrial Grease" and took it over to Biggles. He took a sniff and soon we were all roaring with helpless laughter and Ginger was doing his rear-gunner impersonation and Algy was licking some solvent off my leg and the hangar was beginning to hum. It was a wonderful night, until Biggles suggesting sticking some bombs on to the Jupiter and going to flatten Stevenage. That was when I knew this was getting too heavy for me so I rushed out, grabbing what remained of my clothing, and made for the nearest phone box, where I rang the *Arsehole of the World* and sold the story in desperation.

And now, the Rev. 'Wrinkly' Robags is proud to present the first ever reproduction of the shortest of the gospels describing the birth of our Lord Jesus Christ, recently discovered near the Red Sea.

Gospel According to a Sheep

CHAPTER 1

AND it came to pass that it was a day much like any other. And we were eating grass.

2 And eating more grass. And then moving over and eating another bit of grass.

3 And standing around, looking like we were about to eat another bit of grass.

4 And then doing exactly that: eating another bit of grass.

5 And suddenly, an angel of the Lord appeared, and the glory of the Lord shone around, and we stopped eating for a moment.

6 And the angel said, "Be not afraid: for behold, I bring you tidings of great joy which will come to all people;

7 For unto you this day is born in the city of David a Saviour, who is Christ the Lord."

8 And suddenly there was with the angel a multitude of the heavenly host, praising God and saying,

9 "Glory to God in the highest and on earth, peace among men."

10 At which point, since there had been no mention of any extra grass, or anything relevant to sheep, we went back to eating.

11 But the shepherds did go unto Bethlehem and found a child, wrapped in swaddling clothes and laying in a manger.

12 And they were filled with great joy, and rejoiced and said one unto another: "We have seen the Lord: honoured are we amongst the children of Israel: let us celebrate with great feasting."

13 We sheep had been doing that all along of course. I was already well into my six thousand four hundred and thirteenth mouthful of grass that week.

14 And much discussion was there what they should eat at the feast, and finally did they decide upon lamb, for Jesus was the Lamb of God.

15 And so they came back into the field to pick a lamb, but it was not lambing season, so they did look about for a sheep.

16 And they did find one and he was succulent, and he was tasty, and he was killed and eaten that first of all Christmas days.

17 No prizes for guessing which sheep that was. Oh no.

18 There was a lot of "sheep may safely graze" stuff *afterwards*, of course, when they were feeling well fed and holy, but it didn't do me much good.

CHAPTER 2

AND guess what happened to *me* three days later. Nothing.

HERE ENDS THE GOSPEL ACCORDING TO A SHEEP

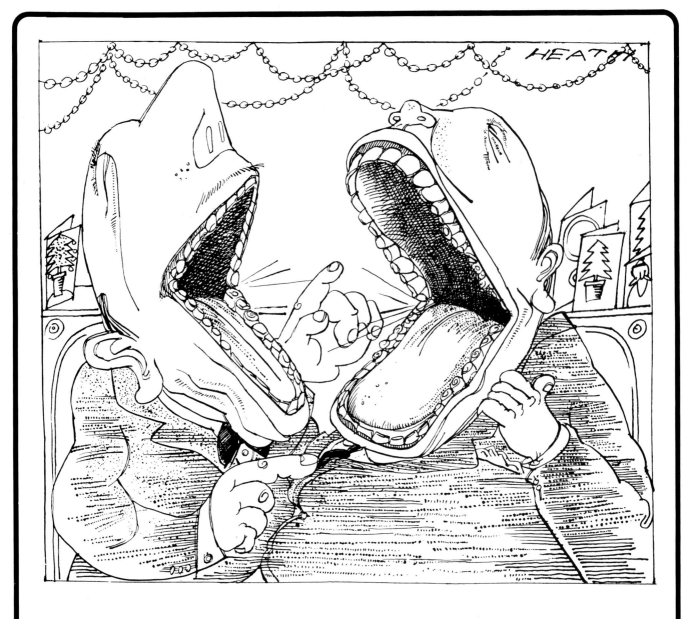

XMAS BORE

I hate it really two weeks sitting around doing nothing we've got to go over to my mother's we're watching the first half of Bridge over the River Kwai there then we're going to her mother's for the second half Jenny's kids are coming of course its her first Christmas on her own since they split up and my brother's coming if he's out of hospital mind you it's not going to be easy they've got the builders in I suppose we'll be watching the Queen at three so we'll have to eat afterwards Jenny won't eat turkey anyway and Geoff's meant to be dropping in but we can't wait for him Mother wants to go to Midnight Mass we never miss it unfortunately last year my sister wrote off the car then there's drinks at Barry's on Boxing Day which means leaving the kids with the neighbours and I've got tickets for Mother Goose with Jimmy Tarbuck I think and the twins are looking forward to it anyway I don't mind you need a bit of a break I find just to unwind I love it really . . .

LADIES, YES IT'S HERE
The brand new Album from
Theophilus P. Wildebeeste

Love Torpedo

Theophilus P. Wildebeeste

Tracks include:
Jump My Bones
Your Tongue In My Ear
Peanut Butter Lover
More Chalk, More Chalk
Paper Bag
Baby Oil Blues
Nighttime Lover, Daytime Accountant
Slave To Open-toed Sandals
Drink My Jacuzzi

And why not get these other Classic Albums?

		Catalogue Number
Theophilus P Wildebeeste		HARD ONE
Just Theo		TRY 69
The P is for Penetration		KINK ONE Y

A MESSAGE TO MY FANS

Hey ladies,
Listen to this Album and your life will never be the same again. It'll make all your juices flow, and I'm not talking about Vitamin C. I'm talking about Vitamins S, E & X. I think you know what I'm trying to say.

This Album was recorded under great pressure – in the sweat box at Pasadena Women's Corrective Centre – Thanks for having me. I think you know where I'm coming from.

Hope you enjoy this Album as much as I enjoy <u>making it.</u>

Love, passion and moistness,

Theophilus xxx

A CHRISTMAS DREAM

A NEW DECADE OF HEROIC FAILURES

by Stephen Pile
with cartoons by Bill Tidy

PREFACE

Getting into the **Guinness Book of Records** is easy. All you have to do is jump over one more Messerschmitt than the last man or eat an extra record-breaking grape. But to get into the **Book of Heroic Failures** by contrast is very, very hard. In the world of the worst there are proven geniuses operating and the standards are so much higher.

In some categories it is difficult to see how anyone could improve upon the existing record. I feel sorry, quite frankly, for a young person nowadays setting out to become the world's worst hijacker when advanced practitioners like the Detroit Two are still airborne. (They threatened the pilot with a plastic knife and said "Take us to Detroit." Glancing up from the controls, he replied "We're already going to Detroit," whereupon these giants of hijacking said "Oh good" and returned to their seats.)

But humanity is an inventive bunch of bipeds, moving ever onwards and downwards. And so on this festive occasion I am pleased to review a decade of solid achievement in our sphere.

First of all we must applaud a new all-time great who now ranks alongside the immortals.

THE SMALLEST AUDIENCE

In August 1980 Joan Melu, a Rumanian folk singer, broke all existing records for the smallest ever audience. Effortlessly pushing aside the previous contenders, he drew an audience of none whatsoever for a concert of what he described as his own style of country and western. Arriving on stage at the Capitol Theatre, Melbourne, in dark glasses and casual clothing, he gazed down on 2,200 empty seats and gave a two-hour show which ran over by 30 minutes.

Throughout Mr Melu performed as if people were there. Coming back on stage after a 5-minute interval the singer announced over the speaker system: "Ladies and gentlemen, Joan Melu." Towards the end of the performance he asked: "Hey everybody, do you want to hear my new one?"

After the show he said that he was "a little nervous" beforehand, but felt very satisfied

IT WAS HARDLY WORTH TURNING THE HEATING UP TO SELL THE CHOC ICES!

with the way it had gone. "I love this life," the artist commented.

According to a stagehand, Mr Melu perched on a stool one metre from the edge of the stage and did not move for two hours except to strum his guitar without any attempt at chords and to mumble into the microphone in a monotone fashion. "Every song appeared the same, musically and vocally."

Faced with this criticism, the singer said that he doesn't pay too much attention to the music because "life is in the song not the notes."

Mr Melu's triumph came during the tour of Australia's largest theatres. The week before he had hired the Sydney Opera House and attracted an audience of 18 plus the *New York Times* music critic, most of whom left before the interval.

THE WORST DRIVER

Few motorists have shown quite so much natural confidence on the road as Miss Bessie Cash who graced Oldham with her skills until 1982 when she voluntarily handed in her driving licence for her own safety.

After 40 years with a clean motoring record, Miss Cash, who was 79, suddenly pulled something extra out of the bag. Although travelling a customary route to her home address in Grange Avenue, she suddenly took the wrong turning and went down a cul-de-sac, on to the pavement, past 13 shop fronts, down a subway, through a labyrinth of tunnels, up into a shopping precinct, down another subway, in and out of some trees, narrowly missing 43 shoppers and Miss Eunice Gerrard, a traffic warden, up on to another pavement, in and out of some more trees and straight into a policeman who tried to stop her, but jumped out of the way and watched her drive past a "No entry" sign and right into a panda car. This brought her to the road she had been looking for.

Of her driving Miss Gerrard, the traffic warden said: "I saw a green mini going down the subway. I thought. 'No, it can't be.' I ended up chasing it in and out of the trees."

Explaining the incident, Miss Cash said afterwards: "I just lost my way." Realising that she could not improve upon this performance, she handed in her licence and has not driven again.

THE LEAST SUCCESSFUL SANTA CLAUS

In 1983 happy children had just left Santa's grotto amidst much yo-ho-hoing when police

walked in, clapped Father Christmas in handcuffs and frogmarched him out through the toy department at Allders store in Croydon. Amazed goblins who assist in the grotto said that Santa was "taken to the police station and charged with persistent non-payment of fines."

While pleading guilty to all the charges at Brighton magistrates court Santa said of his arrest: "It was bloody terrible. I did not like the way it was done." He gave his address as "a bed and breakfast hotel in Streatham".

OXFORD AND CAMBRIDGE BOAT RACE: A NEW RECORD

Cambridge have shot into the lead in the boat race. In 1983 the crews were level, having each sunk three times. (Cambridge showed the way in 1857 and 1978, but valiant Oxford saved their face in 1925 and 1981.)

But then in 1984 pioneering Cambridge did the impossible and sank before the race began. Twenty minutes from the start they rowed into a moored tug and split their own boat in half.

Full of admiration the race umpire, Mr Michael Sweeny, observed, "The cox is only small and he is sitting behind big men. He must have been unsighted."

For sheer style this rivals the great 1912 race in which both boats sank. Oxford went under first and made for the bank. Once the boat had been emptied of water, they could not restart because a brilliant oarsman had disappeared into the crowd to chat with a friend. Some while later he returned and told his disbelieving crew mates that it was "my chum Boswell".

Oxford then saw Cambridge go by, but they were swimming and their boat was nowhere visible. Sadly, this fine race was abandoned just as it was getting interesting.

THE LEAST SUCCESSFUL HOME REPAIRS

Home repairs offer an immense scope to the right sort of person. In 1980 Mr Brian Heise of Utah showed the way when he woke to find a burst pipe flooding his house.

Deciding to hire a pump, he went out to his car only to see that a tyre was flat. Returning indoors to make a phone call, he was hurled

LOOKS LIKE THE BOAT'S READY, SO, TOODLE-PIP, BOSWELL, OLD CHUM!

across the room by an electric shock so great that he ripped the telephone out of the wall.

He then found the dampness had caused the floor to swell and the front door was jammed so he couldn't get out. A seminal figure in the world of home repairs, he spent some while screaming through the window for help. Only when a neighbour smashed down the front door did Mr Heise notice that his car had been stolen.

Having informed the police, hired a pump, sealed the leak and cleaned up his flat, Mr Heise felt that the moment had come for him to relax. Displaying an impressive versatility, he went to a nearby civil war pageant and within minutes of arrival he sat on a bayonet. So he went home where the damp carpet made him come out in a rash. Attempting to take it up, he fell on his bayonet wound and called the doctor who was unable to come because of a terrible traffic jam.

At this point Mr Heise went to bed, having achieved enough for one day.

THE LEAST SUCCESSFUL GETAWAY

A bank robber in Malta set a new world best when he raided the Bank of Valetta, held up the staff, seized the cash, rushed out, dashed across the road and waited at the bus stop for fifteen minutes. During this patient vigil he was arrested by a passing policeman whose suspicions were aroused by the three thousand new banknotes he clasped to his chest.

But in 1976 Mr Alfred Rivera showed what is possible using more conventional methods. During a raid that involved split-second timing Mr Rivera robbed a bar in San Fernando. He dashed out and sprinted down the road to a prearranged meeting place where he was knocked over by his own getaway car.

LEAST SUCCESSFUL ATTEMPT TO CLEAR MOLE HILLS

Tired of the ten large molehills that flourished on his lawn, Mr Oscar Ejiamike decided to remove them. After a vigorous campaign of bombing, gassing and waiting round in the dark with a raised shovel, he found that the ten molehills survived intact. There were also twenty-two new ones.

At this point our man decided to "surprise the moles" with a midnight poisoning raid. He drove his Jaguar 2.4 automatic to the edge of the lawn and trained the headlamps upon the enemy zone. While reaching across for the poison, Mr Ejiamike knocked the car into reverse and accelerated at 60 mph through the wall of his cottage knocking over the electric heater, bursting his petrol tank, setting fire to his newly decorated sitting room, and wrecking his car.

While this certainly surprised the moles, it had no effect upon the 32 molehills amongst which it was little more than a talking point. Next morning Mr Ejiamike bought 22 bags of ready-mixed cement and announced that he was going to concrete the lawn over.

THE LEAST SUCCESSFUL WEDDING RECEPTION

Newlyweds John and Barbara Besio claimed this record at the Blue Dolphin restaurant, Los Angeles, during 1980.

The reception made a promising start when the groom's father expressed the wish to dance upon the table. So unbridled was this performance that the manager called the police. In the resulting fracas five policemen were injured and six wedding guests arrested.

At this point the bride asked what kind of family she was marrying into, whereupon the groom departed from the usual custom, picked up the entire wedding cake and pushed it in her face. When fighting broke out between the happy couple, the police were called again and threatened to arrest them. Guests waving off the happy couple in the going-away car noticed that Mrs Besio, as we must now call her, landed a blow which appeared to temporarily stun her husband, bringing peace to an otherwise perfect occasion.

THE WORST FILM

In the history of the cinema the World's Worst Film Festival proved a highspot. Delegates to this treasure house of special celluloid moments got off to a cracking start with *Tiny Town*, the world's first all-midget Western. It mainly consisted of cowboys walking under saloon doors, chasing each other under bar-room tables and riding into the sunset on what were obviously Shetland ponies. Applause broke out in the chase sequence when the three-foot nine-inch hero "Rocky" Curtis pursued the three-foot eight-inch villain Little Billy. Rocky galloped out of town on a black horse, and was next seen scooting along on a white one only to arrive at his ranch reunited with/back on the black one again.

For six days the festival maintained this high standard and special acclaim went to *The Attack of the Killer Tomatoes*, a four-hour epic in which a consignment of giant tomatoes go berserk and terrorize San Diego. In one of the best scenes a housewife is threatened by a bloodthirsty seedless oozing out of her in-sink garbage grinding unit.

The eventual winner was *They Saved Hitler's Brain* in which the Fuehrer's grey cells wreak post-bunker havoc on a scale that would have surprised even Adolf.

THE LEAST SUCCESSFUL NEWSPAPER COMPETITION

In May 1986 the distinguished British journalist Henry Porter revealed that he had planned five deliberate grammatical errors in his *Sunday Times* column and would send a bottle of champagne to any reader who spotted them all correctly.

Letters poured in by the sackload. The next week Mr Porter announced that readers had found not one of the five mistakes. However they had located a further 23 of which Mr Porter was not aware.

This overtakes the previous best. In 1964 the *Carmel Independent* printed a school photograph and asked readers to identify which child became a well-known celebrity. While cropping the picture for publication, an enthusiastic sub-editor cut out the child in question, making it impossible to win the contest from merely looking at the paper.

Congratulations to all concerned.

A Christmas Fairly Story

By Terry Jones and Douglas Adams

It was Christmas Eve in the future.

Everywhere the snow was falling — down the stairs, out of sixth-floor windows, off ledges and over things lying on the pavement. Crash, bang, bang, cronk! Kerplatt! — it went.

"Snow's jolly heavy today," said Sarah. "And big . . . some of those flakes are fifteen feet across! You never used to get that sort of thing in the past, or even in the present. I wonder . .." But no one would ever know what it was she wondered because, sadly, a snowflake landed on her and she ceased wondering about it, or about anything else ever again.

"Don't grumble, dear," murmured her mother, hurrying to get away from the snow. But it was too late! Three huge flakes screamed down out of the air on her with incredible ferocity. Her last thought before they hit her was "I must make Dennis his sandwiches." Who Dennis was we shall never know, but he certainly wasn't her husband, whose name was Frank.

And what of Frank?

Well, at that very moment, Frank, unaware of the flakey demise of his wife and daughter, was gazing out of the kitchen window. He was a big fan of the future, but not so much of the new snow.

"Terrible snow," he said.

"Yes," agreed his companion, "it's black and hard as rocks. Not really like snow is it?"

"Perhaps it's coal?" suggested Frank.

"Ha!" snorted his companion, who had no name at all because of some really aggravating mix-up with the Registrar of Births, Marriages and Deaths which still hadn't been sorted out despite the dozens and dozens of letters he had sent, none of which were ever replied to because they appeared to come from no one at all. All this made him an extremely tetchy companion, given to violent outbursts on the subjects of snow, nuclear power, and, for some strange reason to do with his mysterious parents, camiknickers. "That's absolutely bloody nonsense! When did you last see any camiknickers anywhere, let alone falling out of the sky?"

"Don't you mean 'when did I last see coal'?" asked Frank quietly.

"Of course I mean coal," yelled The One Whose Name May Not Be Mentioned Because He Hasn't Got One.

"Well, if you mean coal, then, the last time I saw coal was many, many years ago."

"Exactly," expostulated the nameless one triumphantly, and then had to sit down and rest again, because expostulating triumphantly is much more complicated and tiring than simply saying something. Try it and see. "And do you know <u>why</u>? I'll tell you why — because of all the camiknicker stations."

At this point Frank grew weary of the conversation, because it was nonsense, and went down to his job in the vault.

"I meant power stations!" shouted his companion down the steps after him. "I meant nuclear power stations! You know perfectly well I meant the nuclear power stations! You know that when I say camiknickers I really mean camiknickers. I mean . . . oh blast it. I hate the future." But the great steel door to the vault swung closed after Frank, and what the man without a name said was never heard except by a small chaffinch who spoke only Mandarin Chinese and was therefore unable to attach any meaning to his words.

So the nameless one gave up and glumly sat in a chair and stroked his large tumour, which he liked to call Percy.

The reason Frank had a job in a vault was that if you had a job it was best to have a vault to keep it in. Jobs were like gold dust. Better in fact. If you had gold dust you had to keep on hoovering it up and then remembering not to throw it out with the rubbish. But if you had a job, that was really something. Keep it in a vault, that was the best thing.

Frank had a job with one of the most successful and profitable corporations in the world. It did have a name, but it had been changed an awful lot of times. This morning it was called Happiness, Truth and Health, Inc., and it was the public relations company which many years ago had been given the contract to do a campaign to tell people that nuclear power was perfectly safe really.

What a big contract that was!

Boy! With every new nuclear accident that happened, the contract just got bigger and bigger.

The company's stock went through the roof so regularly now that they'd given up having it repaired and just put a pink umbrella over the Stock Exchange. Last year it had completely bought out the other giant Public Relations Company, the United-

Sony-Coca-Cola World Bank of Texaco Comix Corporation (Armaments, Drugs and Origami Division), previously known as the United States of America, so that had been a terrific step forward. Most of the company's employees were now so rich that they could afford to have radiation-proof vaults to keep their jobs in.

Frank rubbed his hands together and eagerly got to work. Today's job was just the sort of one he liked most. Wordcraft, he called it, wordcraft. Last week they had launched a massive campaign to tell people that the huge new nuclear power station that had been built where the Lake District used to be was the safest one ever, this week it had completely blown up, and that called for wordcraft.

A little song maybe, a jingle . . . he got stuck for a while trying to find a rhyme for "colateral damage" and sucked his pencil. "Acceptable tolerances" had a nice ring to it but was rhythmically awkward. No, he had to stress the safety angle. How safe the whole thing was, even in spite of the fact that it had quite clearly exploded. This had been a big accident.

A slight thrill went through him.

Maybe now was the time . . . maybe it had come at last. The big one. Maybe the world was ready. The one he had been saving. The one that said it all. The big one. His baby.

Feverishly he fished in his desk drawer for the key to the little lacquer box he kept in pride of place on his desk. He found it, and fumbling with excitement he opened the box. There lay the piece of paper, neatly folded. He picked it out with trembling fingers, unfolded it, and smoothed it out on the desktop.

He read the few words on it through to himself. He let his breath out slowly.

They were as fine as he remembered them being. Big, bold, irrefutable. Magic. And now at last there had been an accident big enough to be worthy of them.

He reached for the phone.

A few minutes later he emerged from the vault and found his erstwhile companion slumped in a chair, dead. At least that solved the name problem. They could now call him Percy.

He smiled happily to himself and stepped outside. Christmas was in the air, along with a number of other noxious substances. It had stopped snowing now, but the street would probably need some repairs after the afternoon's fall. He threw his hat in the air with pleasure and excitement. I hadn't mentioned that he was wearing a hat, but he was, and this was the hat that he now threw in the air. The reason I hadn't mentioned the hat before was that throwing it in the air is the first interesting thing he has done with it, and I was waiting for that.

Dinner that evening was a little odd. Frank had a vague sense that there was something missing. The Smart-tv sensed his unease, guessed that he would probably like to see something a bit festive and turned itself on.

Frank got himself a can of something fizzy and sat and watched himself having a terrific time being on the Two Complete Assholes Christmas Special. It was great. He hadn't actually been there when it was recorded the previous August, of course, but his Smart-tv knew what Frank looked like and had no trouble mapping him into the picture so he could see what a really wonderful time he was having this Christmas. He relaxed.

After the show came the news.

He looked round to tell his wife to watch, at which point he suddenly realised what it was that was missing. His wife. Sarah. Oh well, he thought, that's what you get for having a nuclear family.

He settled back and watched the reports on the nuclear power station explosion. It had been really huge and was going to make it very difficult to get to Scotland for the foreseeable future, which was a pity what with Hogmanay coming up.

But the Minister explained that because of the number of people who had been colaterally damaged, and the number of jobs that were going to be created by the exciting new project to build a huge tunnel to Scotland, the unemployment figure, seen as a percentage, was going to drop significantly.

"It's an ill wind . . " he joked pleasantly.

The interviewer agreed that it almost certainly was an extreme ill wind indeed, and turned to the question of safety.

"The old, old question," said the Minister with a smile. "I don't know why people keep on about it. I must have said it a million times if I've said it once, it's perfectly perfectly safe!"

"And you say that despite this terrible accident?" asked the interviewer in astonishment.

"I say that because of this not-quite-so-terrible-as-you-make-out accident," smiled the Minister reassuringly. "I say that the fact that we can have an accident like this proves that it's safe."

The interviewer's face dropped. He stuttered.

And the Minister winked. Frank knew that he was winking at him personally, because that was the line he had thought up. He beamed with pride because he knew that there was no answer to that.

Outside a chaffinch sang to say that the story was over.

Radioactive's Christmas Derivations

The station with the reputation for information is proud to present some very exciting Christmas derivations. Mike Channel has been doing long in-depth research, and come up with some real pearls of info, which show just how old pagan rites and other extraneous influences have been blended in with Christian ceremonies to form our Christmas vocabulary.

Mistletoe

The mistletoe kiss originally derives from an ancient Anglo-Saxon custom of cutting off the middle toe on the left foot, to give it to one's loved one. Hence the term 'mistletoe' which is a perversion of the original Anglo-Saxon 'missing toe'. A man and a woman would meet, usually in secret (woodland is symbolised by the hanging plant), and the man would reveal to his loved one that he was missing a toe, at which point she would take him in her arms and embrace him: the missing toe, or 'mistletoe', would be handed over between the teeth as a gesture of love. The habit was eventually replaced by a simple kiss, which performed the same function: also the original tradition was perverted in the fifth century when warriors began to cut off each others' toes as an excuse for a kiss on a cold winter's night.

Turkey

The custom of eating turkey at Christmas apparently dates back to the Middle Ages, when many people, those wealthy enough to celebrate Christmas, still lived in towers, or 'turs'. To open the door to these towers, the heads of large chickens, whose bodies were later to be eaten in the Noel feasting, were forced into the key-holes, and turned, thereby acting as 'keys' to the 'turs', or 'tur-keys'. Once opened the tower would be used for celebration, and the chickens became known as turkeys in recognition of their earlier function.

The Holly & The Ivy

Far from being an ancient carol, this was a song written not about the original plants holly and ivy, but about two pop stars of the early '50s, Buddy Holly and Adam Ivy, a falsetto rhythm and washboard virtuoso. Early competition between the two for hit parade action eventually led to the great fame of Buddy Holly, and the complete disappearance of Adam Ivy. Thus the otherwise difficult lyric:

The Holly and the Ivy
When they are both full grown,
Of all the trees that are in the wood,
The Holly bears the crown.

'The wood' referred to is simply slang for the backwoods where the artists came from. 'Trees' is in fact a perversion of the word 'trio': Buddy Holly was originally supported by his trio, the Crickets, and Adam Ivy by his trio, the Perfumes, an all female bass, sax, comb-and-paper combo. And the 'crown' is of course the crown of the King of Rock 'n' Roll which Buddy Holly held for a while before his tragic death.

Jesus

The word Jesus, far from originally being the name of the Son of God, started as an onomatopoeic word, a word used to represent a sound: in this case the sound of sneezing. (Try it: the word sounds exactly like a rather wet sneeze.) Since the most colds are caught in early December, it became known as the time for catching cold, or Jesus time. This was then combined with the louder variety of sneeze, 'Atchoo', which is how we are left with Jesus, King of the Jews: Jesus, King of 'Atchoo'. No one could have been more surprised than common English folk when this ancient housewives' terminology blended in perfectly with mid-Eastern religious folk-lore: eventually, however, it was taken simply as a further sign of the miraculous powers of the Lord.

Utter lies

Utter lies, such as those above, in fact derive from the old wood flower, the 'utterlee', a kind of lily ('lee') that grew on the outer, or 'utter', edge of a wood. The flowers became connected with complete fabrication as it was the habit of courting couples, who always took to the woods for their misdemeanours, to deny what they had been up to when met by acquaintances on the fringes of the wood, amongst the utterlee flowers. Thus an utterlee became the word for an utter lie.

And now an excerpt from another gospel, recently discovered by the Rev. 'Wrinkly' Robags, this time from the events leading up to the crucifixion of our Lord.

Gospel According to St Sylvester

CHAPTER 23

AND as they led him away, they seized one Simon of Cyrene who was coming in from the country,

8 And laid on him the cross, to carry it behind Jesus.

9 At least they thought it was Simon of Cyrene, but it wasn't. It was a man called Rambo, who was from the U.S. of A. and had come in disguise to deliver Jesus from imprisonment,

10 Which was very much his kind of mission.

11 And when they arrived at the place which was known as Golgotha, or the Place of the Skull, then Rambo did cry out in a loud voice unto the Lord, saying,

12 "Duck!"

13 And the Lord did duck, and, lo, Rambo swung the cross round over the top of his head and knocked out all the Roman centurions.

14 Then he took out a sharp knife and finished them off in the presence of the Lord.

15 And then Jesus spoke to him, saying, "Stop − for this is the Lord's will, that I should be crucified, and that all mankind should be saved."

16 And Rambo said unto him, "Bullshit! That's yellow bellies' talk." And saying so, he knocked out Jesus himself, taking him for a coward. Then did he sling him over his shoulder and head off for Jerusalem.

17 And lo, he went unto the temple, and tore the veil that was in front of the ark of the covenant, and tied it round his head in a bandanna, yelling "Kyre, Kyre, Lama Sabachtani," which was an old football chant, meaning, "Here I come and I'm going to kill anyone foreign."

CHAPTER 24

AND Jesus did come round, and called out, "Forgive him Father, for he knows not what he does."

2 But Rambo did know what he was doing, for he went unto that place where Pilate was, and calling out "Take tha, wop!" did pump him full of lead.

3 And Jesus tried once more to explain that Rambo had completely misunderstood the situation, and if he wasn't crucified, it would change the course of history.

4 And Rambo said, "Yup, that's what I'm here for."

5 And Jesus disassociated himself from the whole caper, and lived happily ever after in Little Rock, Arkansas.

Tiny Tim Strikes Back

By 'Chuck' Dickens

The story so far:

Bob Crachit is in the tyrannous employ of Scrooge, till now the meanest and least generous of men. But a series of apparitions have shown Scrooge the error of his ways, and a great change has come over him. Meanwhile, as the story approaches its climax, the Crachits are sitting down for their meagre Christmas dinner.

They sat down gaily at a table laid with turkey and pudding and all manner of decoration. It was indeed a fine sight to see.

"A fine feast indeed, Mrs Crachit," said Bob merrily. "Would you not agree, Tiny Tim?"

"It certainly is fine," replied Tim, quietly.

"I'd say finer than fine, wouldn't you, Tiny Tim?" repeated Bob with a smile as long as a sausage.

"Yes indeed, I would say that, I certainly would say that," replied Tim. "In fact I will say it. It is finer than fine. There, satisfied?"

"Well, enough of the talking of it, let's have more of the eating," said Mrs Crachit, quite worn out with the fulsomeness of the praise before so much as a morsel had been munched.

"Yes, indeed," said Bob. "And perhaps Tiny Tim would say grace. What do you say, Tiny Tim? Before this huge meal, a tiny grace from our Tiniest of Tims."

Tim did not reply. Clearly, thought Bob, he was thinking too much of eating the food to be planning a grace for it.

"Lost for words, Tiny Tim?" said Bob a little louder.

Again, Tim did not reply.

"Come on," said Bob once more, and louder still. "Not going to give us a special grace for Christmastide, dearest Tiny Tim?"

"Of course I'll give a sodding grace, if you want one," replied Tiny Tim, "but I wish you'd just SHUT UP calling me Tiny Tim all the bloody time. All right, so I'm short, I'm short, let's just leave it at that. I would have thought it was bad enough my being a cripple and going about all day on these crutches without EVERYONE, ENDLESSLY BANGING ON about me being so bloody tiny. Do you think it's nice being short, do you think I actually like looking everyone straight in the groin instead of the eyes. I mean for Christ's sake, just cut out the Tiny Tim stuff, all right. My name's Tim, Timothy to people I don't really know, and Master Crachit to strangers: not Short Tim, or Big Tim or Cripped Tim and most of all, not bloody Tiny Tim. One more Tiny Tim and I smash this house to smithereens, okay? These crutches are weapons and I'm not afraid to use them if this Tiny shit goes on one second longer."

A rather lengthy silence ensued. It had been an unexpected outburst, and Mrs Crachit was most taken aback by some of the vocabulary. But Bob was not a man to let a day be spoiled by some tiny mishap.

"Very well, then . . ." He paused . . . "Tim," he continued, "very well then, plain old Tim, will you say us a grace?"

"Yes I will," said Tim, with a slight smile.

"Three cheers for Tiny Tim," yelled Mrs Crachit, overjoyed that the storm was past.

Tim's hands gripped the crutch and his knuckles turned white with fury.

"O, puss puss, forgive me, milawky and codoodles what a muddleheaded old wombat I am," cried Mrs C. quickly. "Three cheers for Tim, whatever height he be!!"

"That's better," said Tim, loosing his steel grip on the walnut weapon, and bowing his head for grace. "May God bless us each and every one."

"May he indeed," said Bob and began to serve out the delicious bird that had been sitting quite forlorn and ignored during this curious interlude. But what a merry scene was there now, what with the joking and jesting, and the munching, and the calling Tiny Tim "Tim": never had there been such mirth. The only cloud hanging over them was the fact that Bob had been dismissed by Scrooge the day before and they wouldn't ever be able to afford Christmas again.

But then, that instant, the door flew open and who should be standing there but Scrooge himself.

But it was not the Scrooge of old. No more the black pantaloons and dark expression of hate. Instead, there before them stood the merriest of old gentlemen, wearing a cherry waistcoat and scarlet kerchief and a smile as long as a kipper. And in his arms, a veritable cornucopia of gifts.

"Merry Christmas, one and all!" he cried.

Bob was quite lost for words.

"Ha! My dear old friend Bob," laughed Scrooge, "I've seen the error of my ways. Tomorrow you start work for me again, but at double the salary and as a full partner in the firm of Scrooge and Crachit. And here, to be getting on with, is a new quill pen, and for you Mrs Crachit a new pinafore, for that one I see is quite covered in lard. And look, for you Polly, a lovely doll."

Never had there been such joy. Presents of a quality that the Crachits had never seen, let alone possessed, flowed over their tiny room. They could not walk for wrapping papers. Until finally, only one gift remained, quite the largest and heaviest and most expensive of them all.

"And I'll be betting you'll be wondering what this one is," said Scrooge with a merry twinkle in his eyes.

"We certainly are," said Bob, scarce believing there could be any more gifts left in the world to be given.

"Well," said Scrooge, it being quite the happiest moment in his life. "It's the largest gift of all for you, you, my dearest Tiny Tim."

"I'm not fucking Tiny Tim," screamed the psychotic dwarf who had struck him. "Get that into your head and get it good."

But nothing would ever go into Scrooge's head again. He was dead, quite, quite dead.

"O dear," said Mrs Crachit, for rather a pall had certainly been cast over the happy proceedings.

"Yes, O dear, O dear," added Bob, quite crestfallen.

Had it not been for the excellent plum pudding the day would never have recovered. But the pudding was indeed excellent, and candles were lit, and good times were had by all. And Tim was never Tiny again.

He never knew what hit him. The crutch smashed into the side of his head with a crack that sounded like the felling of an oak tree. Scrooge fell to the ground, blood cascading from the temple where he'd been hit and the back of his head where it had smashed against the iron fire grill in the shape of a duck.

LETTER TO MR LIONEL BART ESQ.

Dear Mr Bart,

When Mr. Richard first mentioned the idea of me recording your composition "Living Doll" with him I eagerly accepted- not because I'm completely bloody desperate for work or anything like that of course, but because as a fellow artiste and Thespian (ha,ha that sound's a bit rude dosn't it everybody?) I respect and admire him especiallyb the gaeat way he moves his hips in the WIRED FOR SOUND Vid.

Ho wever when I had a chance to peruse the song more closely I began to have serious doubts about the sexual politics expressed in the lyrics. Later discussions with the Men Againsst Sexism in 12" Disco Remixes.Society merely served to confirm my earlier suspiciams. Really Linel- Cliff was to young to know the difference in 1959, but you should know better. I enclose a rather good critique of your song and some suggested changes which I would like you to make before I can give my hole-hearted consent to them project.

    Yours, Rick

PS. If you ever decide to stage"Oliver"again I know all the words to Food Glorixous Food and most of the dance steps.   P T O

Living Doll – a Feminist Critique.

Got[1] myself[2] a[3] crying[4], talking[5], sleeping walking[6] living[7] doll[8].
Got[9] to do my best to please her, just cos she's a Living Doll.
Got a roving eye and that is why she satisfies my soul.
Got the one and only walking talking Living Doll.

Take a look at her hair: it's real
If you don't elieve what I say just feel
Gonna lock her up in a trunk,
So no big hunk,
Can steal her away from me.

NOTES

I. 'Got': trouble here at the very first word. You have not 'got' the person in question at all. She is a free, independant spirit, making her own choices, her own decisions, and can't be 'got' by anyone. You've 'got' yourself an attitude problem matey, that's what you've got.

2. 'Myself': Preety dicey second word as well. It's all self, self, self with you charvinists, isn't nt? You won't catch me using words ike that – I have much more important things to concern me, I can tell you.

3. 'a': Nothing much wrong here, thank God, though it is a little dismissive.

4. 'crying': TYPICAL, abso-bloody-lutely TYPICAL, (not that there 's anything wrong with blood of course) How many times have you actually seen a woman cry? Well, okay, all right, lots of times – but what makes her cry – your stupidity, that's what!! And anyway, you'd cry too if you had really horrible disgusting things like periods, yeuch!

5. 'talking': TYPICAL: Really – you types are the blummen limit. Many persons of the female persuasion are beautiful vessels of silent thought – and when they are talking you should listen – you might learn something about the struggle in Northern Ireland.

6. 'walking': For flip's sake, Lionel, not all chicks totter round on stilettos. I know you don't actually mention stilettos, but it's implied isn't it? It's all ther in the subtext. I bet you're the sort of person who really likes walking rown along behind girls watching their calf muscles bulging and their botties wiggling up and down in that really exviting way that's really graet? You are, aren't you, you pervy bastard??? And what about the outline of the elastic of their miniscule panties which move sinuously and just visible under their tight skirts to really get you in a froth!!! Just watch it, or rather don't! Euuurgh, where's my hanky?

7. 'livin ': and I suppose she's meant to thank you for that as well! I expect you think she should be bloody grateful that Bill Sykes hasn't jumped her in an alley! She probably should be grateful that you haven't jumped her in an alley yourself what with all that penties stuff you were getting so worked up about. You should be ashamed, you song writers, just trying to get people worked up, well it won't work with me, matey, I can tell you that for free, so sod off with all this silky damp heaving beknickered but not for long buttocks and stocking tops stuff, I won't listen to anymore of it!!! Just shut up!!!

8. 'doll': too cross to say anything about this work actually. In fact, too blinking exhausted to go on with an y of this. I mean, what would you expect when your next line is .....

9. 'got to do my best to please her just cos she's a living doll'. You've got to do your best to please her just because she's a person in her own right and doesn't want you fumbling in her lingerie thank you very much, Lionel. And that's just the chorus! We haven't even got to all the kinky S&M stuff about locking her up in a trunk! You should be bloody graefful l don't get the full
majesty of the Sexy Discrimination Squad on your back, matey! They'd soon ....., well never mind what they'd do, Lionel, I'm sure when you read my lovely new version you'll agree that you can be both feministically acceptable and fun.

Here it is. - - -

the Young ones Nativity Play

And so it came to pass in those days that there went out a decree from Caeser Augustus that all the world should be taxed. And Joseph went up from Galilee into the city of David which is called Bethlehem . . .

And lo, when they were come unto Bethlehem Mary's time was upon her.

And there were in the same country shepherds abiding in the field keeping watch over their flocks by night who saw in the heavens a bright star.

And lo, the Angel of the Lord came upon them and they were sore afraid . . .

And it came to pass that three wise Princes from the East saw the bright star and followed it.

And lo, they found the infant Jesus lying in a table.

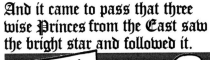

Sorry, a stable . . .

Wrapped in swaddling clothes.

And when they saw the child with Mary his mother they fell down and worshipped Him and presented unto Him gifts of gold, myrrh and frankincense.

And all marvelled at what they saw.

Neil —
My Ten Favourite Things About Christmas

1. It only comes once a year.

2. It only lasts a day.

3. I can't think of anything else.

Mel Smith's
Ten Most Memorable Evenings

1. February 13th 1981
2. 8th June 1971
3. 27th October 1983
4. New Year's Eve —
   February 5th 1984
5. February 7th 1984
6. August 19th 1968
7. August 19th 1969
8. 31st March 1975
9. 2nd April 1980
10. 23 rd July 1986

Two of Shakespeare's Most Rhubarby Sonnets

Shall I compare thee to a piece of rhubarb?
Thou art more lovely and don't have any leaves sticking out of the top.
Rough winds do shake the darling buds of May
And mess up thy hair and also play havoc with the rhubarb,
But that's about the only major point of comparison I can think of.
Rhubarb is much thinner and whippier than thou art,
And doesn't go in and out in such interesting places.
Rhubarb is very good for the digestion and also
For cleaning saucepans, which, with the best will in the world
I have to say that thou, frankly, art not. I know
That I shouldn't automatically expect thee to do them,
And should help out in the kitchen a lot more myself,
But I've got all these plays and sonnets to write.
All in all I think that the answer to the question
Posed in the first line is probably, on reflection,
No. So — on to the next.

Full many a glorious morning have I seen
Flatter the rhubarb patch with sovereign eye.
Oh fuck all this, when's dinner going to be ready?

Christmas Cauliflower

I *wish* it didn't take an hour
To eat a bit of *cauliflower*.

I wish I could gulp the lot
In one go, when it's *hot!*

I wish it didn't get *so* cold....
With *yukky* bits, that look
like *mould*....

I know it makes my Granny grieve,
When I shove it up my sleeve.

And Mum gets in such a flap,
When she spots it in my lap.

And she *always* finds it
later.....

I'd eat it ALL...if I *could*...

Just think of all the poor,
starving children in the
world!

WHAT they'd give
for lovely food
like this!

THEY'D eat your
cauliflower!

I feel like sending
your whole Xmas
dinner straight off
to Africa!

I know of children faraway
With not a thing to eat all day...

My dinner's not enough to share
Among the hungry people there.

<u>*I'd*</u> send them *tons & tons* of chips
And thirty *squillion Instant Whips*,
And mounds of chocolate cake and jam,
And beans & cheese & crisps and Ham-
Burgers...and pies and honey....
...And I'd send my pocket money....

And all these things I'd send
by rocket...

Posy Simmonds

82

Young Zaphod Plays It Safe

A Hitch-Hiker's Guide Short Story

by Douglas Adams

A large flying craft moved swiftly across the surface of an astoundingly beautiful sea. From mid-morning onwards it plied back and forth in great widening arcs, and at last attracted the attention of the local islanders, a peaceful, sea-food loving people who gathered on the beach and squinted up into the blinding sun, trying to see what was there.

Any sophisticated knowledgeable person, who had knocked about, seen a few things, would probably have remarked on how much the craft looked like a filing cabinet — a large and recently burgled filing cabinet lying on its back with its drawers in the air and flying.

The islanders, whose experience was of a different kind, were instead struck by how little it looked like a lobster.

They chattered excitedly about its total lack of claws, its stiff unbendy back, and the fact that it seemed to experience the greatest difficulty staying on the ground. This last feature seemed particularly funny to them. They jumped up and down on the spot a lot to demonstrate to the stupid thing that they themselves found staying on the ground the easiest thing in the world.

But soon this entertainment began to pall for them. After all, since it was perfectly clear to them that the thing was not a lobster, and since their world was blessed with an abundance of things that were lobsters (a good half a dozen of which were now marching succulently up the beach towards them)

they saw no reason to waste any more time on the thing but decided to adjourn immediately for a late lobster lunch.

At that exact moment the craft stopped suddenly in mid-air then upended itself and plunged headlong into the ocean with a great crash of spray which sent them shouting into the trees.

When they re-emerged, nervously, a few minutes later, all they were able to see was a smoothly scarred circle of water and a few gulping bubbles.

That's odd, they said to each other between mouthfuls of the best lobster to be had anywhere in the Western Galaxy, that's the second time that's happened in a year.

—·—

The craft which wasn't a lobster dived direct to a depth of two hundred feet, and hung there in the heavy blueness, while vast masses of water swayed about it. High above, where the water was magically clear, a brilliant formation of fish flashed away. Below, where the light had difficulty reaching, the colour of the water sank to a dark and savage blue.

Here, at two hundred feet, the sun streamed feebly. A large, silk-skinned sea-mammal rolled idly by, inspecting the craft with a kind of half-interest, as if it had half expected to find something of this kind round about here, and then it slid on up and away towards the rippling light.

The craft waited here for a minute or two, taking

◆

readings, and then descended another hundred feet. At this depth it was becoming seriously dark. After a moment or two the internal lights of the craft shut down, and in the second or so that passed before the main external beams suddenly stabbed out, the only visible light came from a small hazily illuminated pink sign which read *The Beeblebrox Salvage and Really Wild Stuff Corporation*.

The huge beams switched downwards, catching a vast shoal of silver fish, which swivelled away in silent panic.

In the dim control room which extended in a broad bow from the craft's blunt prow, four heads were gathered round a computer display that was analysing the very, very faint and intermittent signals that were emanating from deep on the sea bed.

"That's it," said the owner of one of the heads finally.

"Can we be quite sure?" said the owner of another of the heads.

"One hundred per cent positive," replied the owner of the first head.

"You're one hundred per cent positive that the ship which is crashed on the bottom of this ocean is the ship which you said you were one hundred per cent positive could one hundred per cent positively never crash?" said the owner of the two remaining heads. "Hey," he put up two of his hands, "I'm only asking."

The two officials from the Safety and Civil Reassurance Administration responded to this with a very cold stare, but the man with the odd, or rather the even number of heads, missed it. He flung himself back on the pilot couch, opened a couple of beers — one for himself and the other also for himself — stuck his feet on the console and said "Hey, baby" through the ultra-glass at a passing fish.

"Mr Beeblebrox . . ." began the shorter and less reassuring of the two officials in a low voice.

"Yup?" said Zaphod, rapping a suddenly empty can down on some of the more sensitive instruments, "you ready to dive? Let's go."

"Mr Beeblebrox, let us make one thing perfectly clear . . ."

"Yeah let's," said Zaphod, "How about this for a start. Why don't you just tell me what's really on this ship?"

"We have told you," said the official. "By-products."

Zaphod exchanged weary glances with himself.

"By-products," he said. "By-products of what?"

"Processes," said the official.

"What processes?"

"Processes that are perfectly safe."

"Santa Zarquana Voostra!" exclaimed both of Zaphod's heads in chorus, "so safe that you have to build a zarking fortress ship to take the by-products to the nearest black hole and tip them in! Only it doesn't get there because the pilot does a detour — is this right? — to pick up some *lobster* . . .? OK, so the guy is cool, but . . . I mean own up, this is barking time, this is major lunch, this is stool approaching critical mass, this is . . . this is . . . *total vocabulary failure!*"

"Shut *up!*" his right head yelled at his left, "we're *flanging!*"

He got a good calming grip on the remaining beer can.

"Listen guys," he resumed after a moment's peace and contemplation. The two officials had said nothing. Conversation at this level was not something to which they felt they could aspire. "I just want to know," insisted Zaphod, "what you're getting me into here."

He stabbed a finger at the intermittent readings trickling over the computer screen. They meant nothing to him but he didn't like the look of them at all. They were all squiggly with lots of long numbers and things.

"It's breaking up, is that it?" he shouted. "It's got a hold full epsilonic radiating aorist rods or something that'll fry this whole space sector for zillions of years back and it's breaking up. Is that the story? Is that what we're going down to find? Am I going to come out of that wreck with even *more* heads?"

"It cannot possibly be a wreck, Mr Beeblebrox," insisted the official, "the ship is guaranteed to be perfectly safe. It cannot possibly break up."

"Then why are you so keen to go and look at it?"

"We like to look at things that are perfectly safe."

"Freeeooow!"

"Mr Breeblebrox," said an official, patiently, "may I remind you that you have a job to do?"

◆

"Yeah, well maybe I don't feel so keen on doing it all of a sudden. What do you think I am, completely without any moral whatsits, what are they called, those moral things?"

"Scruples?"

"Scruples, thank you, whatsoever? Well?"

The two officials waited calmly. They coughed slightly to help pass the time.

Zaphod sighed a "what is the world coming to" sort of sigh to absolve himself from all blame, and swung himself round in his seat.

"Ship?" he called.

"Yup?" said the ship.

"Do what I do."

The ship thought about this for a few milliseconds and then, after double checking all the seals on its heavy duty bulkheads, it began slowly, inexorably, in the hazy blaze of its lights, to sink to the lowest depths.

— · —

Five hundred feet.

A thousand.

Two thousand.

Here, at a pressure of nearly seventy atmospheres, in the chilling depths where no light reaches, nature keeps its most heated imaginings. Two foot long nightmares loomed wildly into the bleaching light, yawned, and vanished back into the blackness.

Two and a half thousand feet.

At the dim edges of the ship's lights guilty secrets flitted by with their eyes on stalks.

Gradually the topography of the distantly approaching ocean bed resolved with greater and greater clarity on the computer displays until at last a shape could be made out that was separate and distinct from its surroundings. It was like a huge lopsided cylindrical fortress which widened sharply halfway along its length to accommodate the heavy ultra-plating with which the crucial storage holds were clad, and which were supposed by its builders to have made this the most secure and impregnable spaceship ever built. Before launch the material structure of this section had been battered, rammed, blasted and subjected to every assault its builders knew it could withstand in order to demonstrate that

it could withstand them.

The tense silence in the cockpit tightened perceptibly as it became clear that it was this section that had broken rather neatly in two.

"In fact it's perfectly safe," said one of the officials, "it's built so that even if the ship does break up, the storage holds cannot possibly be breached."

— · —

Three thousand, eight hundred and twenty-five feet.

Four Hi-Presh-A SmartSuits moved slowly out of the open hatchway of the salvage craft and waded through the barrage of its lights towards the monstrous shape that loomed darkly out of the sea night. They moved with a sort of clumsy grace, near-weightless though weighed on by a world of water.

With his right-hand head Zaphod peered up into the black immensities above him and for a moment his mind sang with a silent roar of horror. He glanced to his left and was relieved to see that his other head was busy watching the Brockian Ultra-Cricket broadcasts on the helmet vid without concern. Slightly behind him to his left walked the two officials from the Safety and Civil Reassurance Administration, slightly in front of him to his right walked the empty suit, carrying their implements and testing the way for them.

They passed the huge rift in the broken-backed Starship Billion Year Bunker, and played their flashlights up into it. Mangled machinery loomed between torn and twisted bulkheads, two feet thick. A family of large transparent eels lived in there now and seemed to like it.

The empty suit preceded them along the length of the ship's gigantic murky hull, trying the airlocks. The third one it tested ground open uneasily. They crowded inside it and waited for several long minutes while the pump mechanisms dealt with the hideous pressure that the ocean exerted, and slowly replaced it with the equally hideous pressure of air and inert gases. At last the inner door slid open and they were admitted to a dark outer holding area of the Starship Billion Year Bunker.

Several more high security Titan-O-Hold doors

◆

had to be passed through, each of which the officials opened with a selection of quark keys. Soon they were so deep within the heavy security fields that the Ultra-Cricket broadcasts were beginning to fade, and Zaphod had to switch to one of the rock video stations, since there was nowhere that they were not able to reach.

A final doorway slid open, and they emerged into a large sepulchral space. Zaphod played his flashlight against the opposite wall and it fell full on a wild-eyed screaming face.

Zaphod screamed a diminished fifth himself, dropped his light and sat heavily on the floor, or rather on a body which had been lying there undisturbed for around six months and which reacted to being sat on by exploding with great violence. Zaphod wondered what to do about all this, and after a brief but hectic internal debate decided that passing out would be the very thing.

He came to a few minutes later and pretended not to know who he was, where he was or how he had got there, but was not able to convince anybody. He then pretended that his memory suddenly returned with a rush and that the shock caused him to pass out again, but he was helped unwillingly to his feet by the empty suit — which he was beginning to take a serious dislike to — and forced to come to terms with his surroundings.

They were dimly and fitfully lit and unpleasant in a number of respects, the most obvious of which was the colourful arrangement of parts of the ship's late lamented Navigation Officer over the floor, walls and ceiling, and especially over the lower half of his, Zaphod's, suit. The effect of this was so astoundingly nasty that we shall not be referring to it again at any point in this narrative — other than to record briefly the fact that it caused Zaphod to throw up inside his suit, which he therefore removed and swapped, after suitable headgear modifications, with the empty one. Unfortunately the stench of the fetid air in the ship, followed by the sight of his own suit walking around casually draped in rotting intestines was enough to make him throw up in the other suit as well, which was a problem that he and the suit would simply have to live with.

There. All done. No more nastiness.

At least, no more of that particular nastiness.

The owner of the screaming face had calmed down very slightly now and was bubbling away incoherently in a large tank of yellow liquid — an emergency suspension tank.

"It was crazy," he babbled, "crazy! I told him we could always try the lobster on the way back, but he was crazy. Obsessed! Do you ever get like that about lobster? Because I don't. Seems to me it's all rubbery and fiddly to eat, and not that much taste, well I mean is there? I infinitely prefer scallops, and said so. Oh Zarquon, I *said* so!"

Zaphod stared at this extraordinary apparation, flailing in its tank. The man was attached to all kinds of life-support tubes, and his voice was bubbling out of speakers that echoed insanely round the ship, returning as haunting echoes from deep and distant corridors.

"That was where I went wrong," the madman yelled, "I actually said that I preferred scallops and he said it was because I hadn't had real lobster like they did where his ancestors came from, which was here, and he'd prove it. He said it was no problem, he said the lobster here was worth a whole journey, let alone the small diversion it would take to get here, and he swore he could handle the ship in the atmosphere, but it was madness, madness!" he screamed, and paused with his eyes rolling, as if the word had rung some kind of bell in his mind. "The ship went right out of control! I couldn't believe what we were doing and just to prove a point about lobster which is really so over-rated as a food, I'm sorry to go on about lobsters so much, I'll try and stop in a minute, but they've been on my mind so much for the months I've been in this tank, can you imagine what it's like to be stuck in a ship with the same guys for months eating junk food when all one guy will talk about is lobster and then spend six months floating by yourself in a tank thinking about it. I promise I will try and shut up about the lobsters, I really will. Lobsters, lobsters, lobsters — enough! I think I'm the only survivor. I'm the only one who managed to get to an emergency tank before we went down. I sent out the Mayday and then we hit. It's a disaster isn't it? A total disaster, and all because the guy liked lobsters. How much sense am I making? It's really hard for me to tell."

He gazed at them beseechingly, and his mind seemed to sway slowly back down to earth like a falling leaf. He blinked and looked at them oddly like a monkey peering at a strange fish. He scrabbled curiously with his wrinkled up fingers at the glass side of the tank. Tiny, thick yellow bubbles loosed themselves from his mouth and nose, caught briefly in his swab of hair and strayed on upwards.

"Oh Zarquon, oh heavens," he mumbled pathetically to himself, "I've been found. I've been rescued . . ."

"Well," said one of the officials, briskly, "you've been found at least." He strode over to the main computer bank in the middle of the chamber and started checking quickly through the ship's main monitor circuits for damage reports.

"The aorist rod chambers are intact," he said.

"Holy dingo's dos," snarled Zaphod, "there *are* aorist rods on board . . !"

Aorist rods were devices used in a now happily abandoned form of energy production. When the hunt for new sources of energy had at one point got particularly frantic, one bright young chap suddenly spotted that one place which had never used up all its available energy was — the past. And with the sudden rush of blood to the head that such insights tend to induce, he invented a way of mining it that very same night, and within a year huge tracts of the past were being drained of all their energy and simply wasting away. Those who claimed that the past should be left unspoilt were accused of indulging in an extremely expensive form of sentimentality. The past provided a very cheap, plentiful and clean source of energy, there could always be a few Natural Past Reserves set up if anyone wanted to pay for their upkeep, and as for the claim that draining the past impoverished the present, well, maybe it did, slightly, but the effects were immeasurable and you really had to keep a sense of proportion.

It was only when it was realised that the present was being impoverished, and that the reason for it was that those selfish plundering wastrel bastards up in the future were doing exactly the same thing, that everyone realised that every single aorist rod, and the terrible secret of how they were made, would have to be utterly and forever destroyed. They claimed it was for the sake of their grandparents and grandchildren, but it was of course for the sake of their grandparents' grandchildren, and their grandchildren's grandparents.

The official from the Safety and Civil Reassurance Administration gave a dismissive shrug.

"They're perfectly safe," he said. He glanced up at Zaphod and suddenly said with uncharacteristic frankness, "There's worse than that on board. At least," he added, tapping at one of the computer screens, "I hope it's on board."

The other official rounded on him sharply.

"What the hell do you think you're saying?" he snapped.

The first shrugged again. He said, "It doesn't matter. He can say what he likes. No one would believe him. It's why we chose to use him rather than do anything official isn't it? The more wild the story he tells, the more it'll sound like he's some hippy adventurer making it up. He can even say that we said this and it'll make him sound like a paranoid." He smiled pleasantly at Zaphod, who was seething in a suit full of sick. "You may accompany us," he told him, "if you wish."

— · —

"You see?" said the official, examining the ultra-titanium outer seals of the aorist rod hold. "Perfectly secure, perfectly safe."

He said the same thing as they passed holds containing chemical weapons so powerful that a teaspoon could fatally infect an entire planet.

He said the same thing as they passed holds containing zeta-active compounds so powerful that a teaspoonful could blow up a whole planet.

He said the same thing as they passed holds containing theta-active compounds so powerful that a teaspoonful could irradiate a whole planet.

"I'm glad I'm not a planet," muttered Zaphod.

"You'd have nothing to fear," assured the official from the Safety and Civil Reassurance Administration, "planets are very safe. Provided," he added — and paused. They were approaching the hold nearest to the point where the back of the *Starship Billion Year Bunker* was broken. The corridor here was twisted and deformed, and the floor was damp and sticky in patches.

"Ho hum," he said, "ho very much hum."

"What's in this hold?" demanded Zaphod.

"By-products" said the official, clamming up again.

"By-products . . ." insisted Zaphod, quietly, "of what?"

Neither official answered. Instead, they examined the hold door very carefully and saw that its seals were twisted apart by the forces that had deformed the whole corridor. One of them touched the door lightly. It swung open to his touch. There was darkness inside, with just a couple of dim yellow lights deep within it.

"Of *what?*" hissed Zaphod.

The leading official turned to the other.

"There's an escape capsule," he said, "that the crew were to use to abandon ship before jettisoning it into the black hole," he said. "I think it would be good to know that it's still there." The other official nodded and left without a word.

The first official quietly beckoned Zaphod in. The large dim yellow lights glowed about twenty feet from them.

"The reason," he said, quietly, "why everything else in this ship is, I maintain, safe, is that no one is really crazy enough to use them. No one. At least no one that crazy would ever get near them. Anyone that mad or dangerous rings very deep alarm bells. People may be stupid but they're not *that* stupid."

"By-products," hissed Zaphod again — he had to hiss in order that his voice shouldn't be heard to tremble — "of what."

"Er, Designer People."

"*What?*"

"The Sirius Cybernetics Corporation were awarded a huge research grant to design and produce synthetic personalities to order. The results were uniformly disastrous. All the 'people' and 'personalities' turned out to be amalgams of characteristics which simply could not co-exist in naturally occuring life forms. Most of them were just poor pathetic misfits, but some were deeply, deeply dangerous. Dangerous because they didn't ring alarm bells in other people. They could walk through situations the way that ghosts walk through walls, because no one spotted the danger.

"The most dangerous of all were three identical ones — they were put in this hold, to be blasted, with this ship, right out of this universe. They are not evil, in fact they are rather simple and charming. But they are the most dangerous creatures that ever lived because there is nothing they will not do if allowed, and nothing they will not be allowed to do . . ."

Zaphod looked at the dim yellow lights, the two dim yellow lights. As his eyes became accustomed to the light he saw that the two lights framed a third space where something was broken. Wet sticky patches gleamed dully on the floor.

Zaphod and the official walked cautiously towards the light. At that moment, four words came crashing into the helmet headsets from the other official.

"The capsule has gone," he said tersely.

"Trace it," snapped Zaphod's companion. "Find exactly where it has gone. We *must* know where it has gone!"

Zaphod slid aside a large round glass door. Beyond it lay a tank full of thick yellow liquid, and floating in it was a man, a kindly looking man with lots of pleasant laugh lines round his face. He seemed to be floating quite contentedly and smiling to himself.

Another terse message suddenly came through his helmet headset. The planet towards which the escape capsule had headed had already been identified. It was in Galactic Sector ZZ9 Plural Z Alpha.

The kindly looking man in the tank seemed to be babbling gently to himself, just as the co-pilot had been in his tank. Little yellow bubbles beaded on the man's lips. Zaphod found a small speaker by the tank and turned it on. He heard the man babbling gently about a shining city on a hill.

He also heard the official from the Safety and Civil Reassurance Administration issue instructions that the planet in ZZ9 Plural Z Alpha must be made "perfectly safe."

Griff Rhys Jones' Favourite Christmas Joke

Now this is very funny, you see. No. Now...Um. Supergirl was flying home one day across the skies, you know as she does, and she saw the Invisible Man...no just a minute, forget I said that. It wasn't Supergirl you see. It was Superman. He was flying home across the skies. I think he was late for a meeting of the Legion of Superheroes or something. Actually, he was

definitely late for the meeting. We should start at the meeting. It gives a bit of colour, don't you think? He was *at* the meeting. Well he wasn't actually there. He arrived late. And he walks in, and another of the Superheroes, like the Wobblyman...Do you know any of the Superheroes at all? Because I never read any of those comics. I was more a Dandy man myself. Anyway, one of those other Superhero people says "Oh Superman, glad to see you've arrived, where have you been?" Because he was late, you see.

So Superman says, "I'm sorry I'm late etc, etc, etc, but while I was flying on my way to this meeting of the Superheroes, who are all there looking at him of course; while I was flying here, who should I see but the Invisible Man.

Oh God. No. I've got that wrong. It wasn't the Invisible Man, it was Supergirl. I knew she was in this somewhere. It was Supergirl. That's who Superman saw when he was flying along . . . Or maybe it was Wonderwoman. Have you heard this before? Well anyway, look, it doesn't really matter because it was some sort of Superlady

and she was lying there. What? No, not at the meeting of Superheroes. This was before. When Superman was flying along on his way there. This is why he was late, you see. It's not really important that he was late, actually, that's just the preamble. The important thing is that he saw this Superlady etc, etc, etc. Anyway, right . . . O.K. He saw this Superlady and she was, well, you know . . . Anyway she hadn't got any of her clothes on, well not the bottom half any-way if you follow my drift . . . and Superman

thought it would be a good idea to . . . so he did, only the Invisible Man was in the way, because he was . . . you know. You don't get it do you? No, that's the punchline. It was the Invisible Man

all the time you see. Superman didn't see him because he was Invisible, being the Invisible

Man of course. So he you know, he put it right up the Invisible Man. Yes . . . of course its not really very Christmassy is it? No. Actually, it's the only joke I know. Ha ha.

Mel Smith's favourite party game.

1. Take seven large bottles of vodka.

2. Pour them into a bucket or suitable receptacle.

3. Drink.

4. Lie on the floor for several hours.

5. Don't Go to bed.

6. Repeat until dead.

CHRISTMAS Crisis KIT

Does Christmas to you mean Hell on Earth, instead of Peace on Earth? Nothing but trouble and unhappiness and embarrassment?

Then you need the exciting new **Comic Relief Crisis Christmas Kit,** specially designed to solve all those awkward Christmas Problems.

So don't delay –
PUT THE KIT TO WORK!

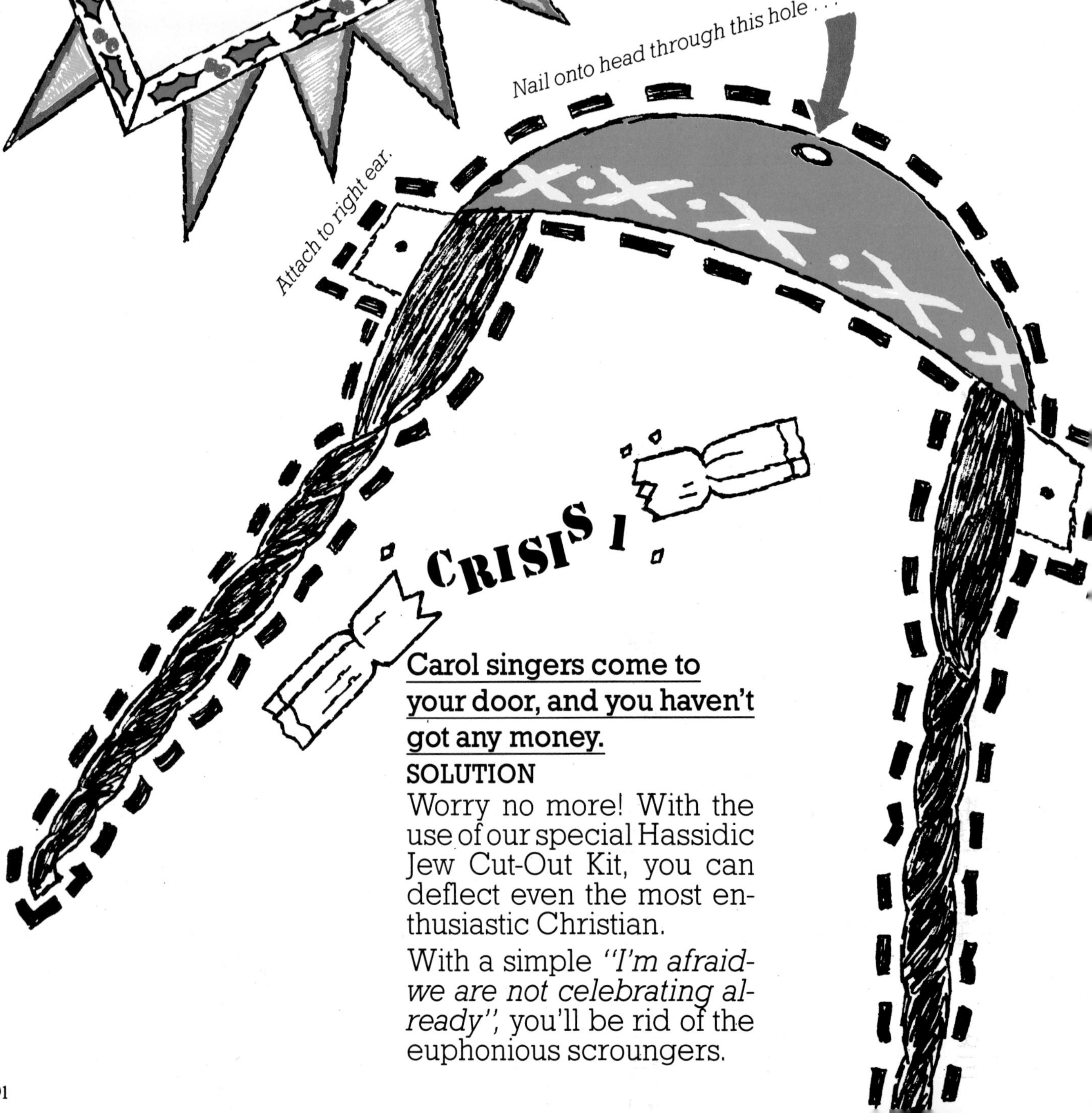

Nail onto head through this hole . . .

Attach to right ear.

CRISIS 1

Carol singers come to your door, and you haven't got any money.

SOLUTION

Worry no more! With the use of our special Hassidic Jew Cut-Out Kit, you can deflect even the most enthusiastic Christian.

With a simple *"I'm afraid we are not celebrating already",* you'll be rid of the euphonious scroungers.

CRISIS 2

You've forgotten to buy a present for your mother.

SOLUTION

This could be a very difficult moment: but not if you take our advice with the invaluable **Grandmother Techniques**

A. If your Grandmother is not with you, and lives alone on the other side of the world, the way out of the problem with your mother's present is to **RING GRANNY**. Every year, you know that your Mother has to force you to ring Grandmother on Christmas Day. So, this year, just when it is your turn to give your present to your mother, say,

"Wait a second though, isn't it about time that we rang darling Granny?" This will be the happiest moment of your mother's life. That you should actually suggest, willingly, to ring the old girl is a miracle greater than all of little baby Jesus' showy numbers with fish. By the time you get back from the phone call (see **Crisis Kit Appendix One: What to Say to Granny**), everyone will have forgotten where you were in the present-giving rota, and, if you grab the initiative, the crisis is averted.

B. If your Grandmother is actually with you, a different technique has to be used. You must revert to plan number two: **KILL GRANNY.**

This is an exceptionally effective distraction. At some point before the moment comes for giving the unbought present to your mother, your grandmother is certain to have to leave the room to do something. You follow her – *"I'll make sure Gran's alright"* — and then quickly kill her. Then come back into the room, yelling, *"Oh God, Oh God, there's been the most dreadful accident!"* The consequent fuss will to a great extent take the heat out of the failure to buy the present. (For further use of Grandmother, see **Crisis Kit Appendix Two: Eating Granny.**)

CRISIS 3

You have no money for Collection.

SOLUTION

The Crisis Kit solves this perennial stinker in an instant with special **Crisis Kit Christmas Money**. Does it look unconvincing and pathetic? Yes, it does – but the doddering gits who collect the money in church aren't going to know the difference, are they?

If, however, your church is one of those awful ones filled with sturdy young keenies in tweed jackets, you can do three things when the plate comes round.

1. Faint. A simple faint will be unconvincing, so go for the whopping great lie – *"It was unbelievable – suddenly in front of the altar I saw the ghost of a little child, in swaddling clothes, and his eyes were shining like stars, etc. etc. etc. . . ."* Then begin to speak in tongues.

2. Steal the money. This however includes an element of risk, so by far the best of all courses is . . .

3. Pretend the money has been stolen from you.

The scenario.

A. The hymn is announced.

B. You nudge the person next to you with a big smile, saying, "Well, at least this year I've remembered my collection money."

C. You reach confidently into your pocket.

D. A look of horror comes over your face and you cry out in a VERY LOUD VOICE INDEED . . .

*"SHIT! – someone's stolen my money! No, really this is OUTRAGEOUS! Christ, what are we coming to when people will actually steal money in church. Vicar! VICAR! I hate to have to stop proceedings like this, but somewhere in this church is a bloody thief, and you and I know how much Jesus hated those kind of people. I came in here, I mean, I wasn't going to tell anyone, I was just going to slip it into the plate, but now I've got to tell you – I came in here with £150! And I put it in my pocket and **some bastard has nicked it.** I mean, I dont mind losing the money, hell, I was going to give it away anyway, but I hope, I really hope that the bastard who nicked it realises that if it weren't for people like him OR HER, we wouldn't have to go through this Christmas service every year because the little baby Jesus wouldn't have had to be born and crucified to save sinners like him, or her, the total and utter bastard!*

(YOU WILL NOTICE WE HAVE SUPPLIED A SPECIALLY PERFORATED CRIB-SHEET THAT WILL CONVENIENTLY FIT INSIDE YOUR HYMNAL.)

The system is foolproof – it also means you can be in a bad mood for the rest of the day, and explains why you have bought such terrible presents for everyone, because you were saving up all your money for the collection, which some total and utter bastard went and nicked.

CRISIS 4

You suddenly realise that all your presents are cheap and nasty.

SOLUTION

This nasty situation is now easily solved by the application of our special **Comic Relief Crisis Kit Price Tags.**

With a little dab of glue, these, tactically stuck to your gifts, should do the trick.

EXTRA EXTRA! BUMPER BONUS!

And in case the gifts given by your brothers or sisters are noticeably classier and more expensive . . .

W
WATERSTONE'S
£25

Harrods
£120

PENHALIGON'S
£55

Benedick, Pooh
& Mumpchkin
Finest Hand-Wrought
Chocolates
£385.95 a quarter

The
John Paul
Getty Museum
£312,000

WOOLWORTHS
SALE ~~35p~~ 8p

WOOLWORTHS
SALE ~~£1~~ 35p

"BUY A PACKET OF THREE, GET THIS FREE"

These tactically placed will soon put paid to the greasy goody-goodies.

CRISIS 5

You have brought no presents at all.

SOLUTION

The only way of getting out of this is the famous **Moustache & Beard Technique.**

You slip out of the house before the present giving and apply one of the moustaches or beards below:

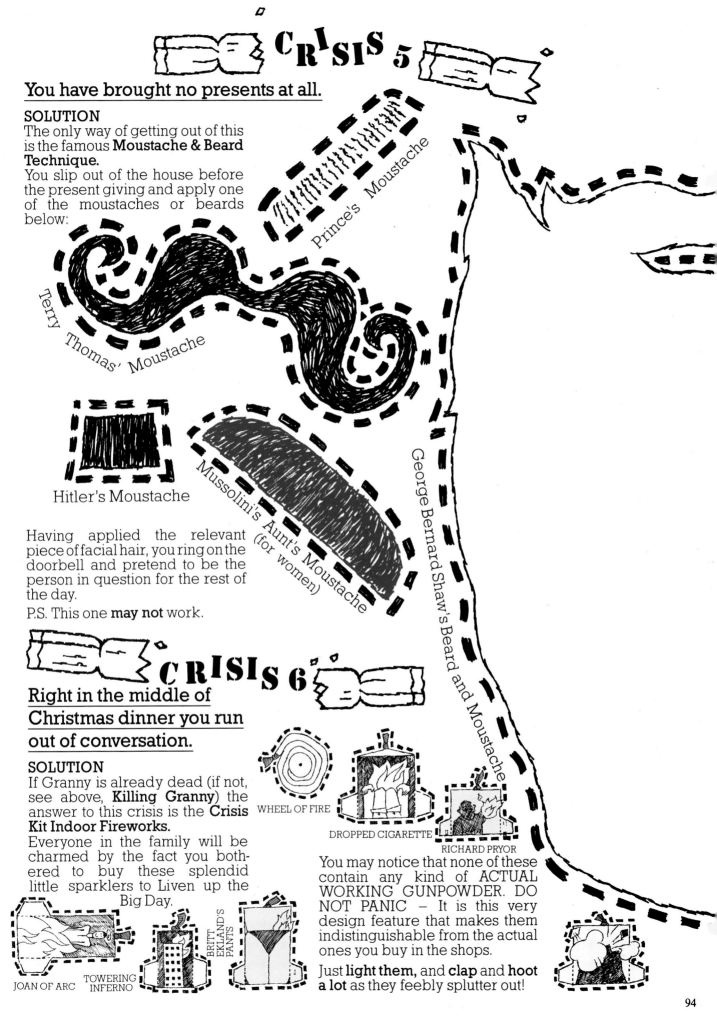

Prince's Moustache

Terry Thomas' Moustache

Hitler's Moustache

Mussolini's Aunt's Moustache (for women)

George Bernard Shaw's Beard and Moustache

Having applied the relevant piece of facial hair, you ring on the doorbell and pretend to be the person in question for the rest of the day.

P.S. This one **may not** work.

CRISIS 6

Right in the middle of Christmas dinner you run out of conversation.

SOLUTION

If Granny is already dead (if not, see above, **Killing Granny**) the answer to this crisis is the **Crisis Kit Indoor Fireworks.**

Everyone in the family will be charmed by the fact you bothered to buy these splendid little sparklers to Liven up the Big Day.

WHEEL OF FIRE

DROPPED CIGARETTE

RICHARD PRYOR

You may notice that none of these contain any kind of ACTUAL WORKING GUNPOWDER. DO NOT PANIC – It is this very design feature that makes them indistinguishable from the actual ones you buy in the shops.

Just **light them,** and **clap** and **hoot a lot** as they feebly splutter out!

JOAN OF ARC

TOWERING INFERNO

BRITT EKLAND'S PANTS

CRISIS '73

The present-giving and the meal are over. At last you can relax. OR CAN YOU?

NO – because there's something you want to watch on one side and you know there's something else that everyone else will want to watch on the other!

SOLUTION

This is the plan . . . You need never worry again with our . . .

SPECIAL CHRISTMAS CRISIS KIT TV STICK-IN SCHEDULES.

Before Christmas Day stick these over the programmes that compete with your chosen viewing schedule.

Then, when the time comes to switch on the TV, make a self-righteous little speech:

"Let's try this year not to have all those awful rows about who watches what, okay folks. So, before we switch it on, let's just plan out our evening viewing, using the TV and Radio Times, and stick to it."

When they see these dreadful alternatives, you will easily be able to win your chosen timetable. **Good luck and Good viewing!**

A Tribute to Bob Monkhouse

A gala tribute to Britain's Most-Loved Entertainer, presented by **Michael Bentine**, Britain's Next-Most-Loved Entertainer.

Produced by **Des O'Connor**

A Tribute to Michael Bentine

A gala tribute to Britain's Next-Most-Loved Entertainer.
Presented by Isla St Clair, Britain's Next-After-That-Most-Loved Entertainer.

Produced by **Nana Mouskouri**

The Steve Davis Story

An exciting 2 hour biofilm on the exciting life of TV's Number One Entertainer, **Steve Davis.**
Starring
BOB MONKHOUSE as Steve Davis
MICHAEL BENTINE as Hurricane Higgins
ISLA ST CLAIR as Ray Rearden
VAL DOONICAN as Dennis Taylor

Directed by **A. Traffic-Warden**

The Very Best of the Open University

A compilation of highlights from the Open University programmes.
Featuring **Geological Structurations, Course 1 & 2 & Phonetics, Priapism & Philology, Grade 3-4.**
Presented by A. Beardy-Wierdy & F. Four-Eyes.

Produced by **A. Bore**

Pebble Mill: The Music

Musical Highlights from Pebble Mill over the years, featuring **Roger Whittaker, Jake Thackeray, The King Singers** and **Roger Whittaker** again, doing a reprise of 'Durham Town'.

Produced by **Mary Hopkins & Cilla Black.**

Your Viscera in Their Bloodied Fingers

Graphic Highlights from All Those Programmes About People Cutting Other People Open.
Featuring **Open Heart Surgery**, and **The Twins Who Swallowed Razorblades.**

Presented by **Doctor Who**
Produced by **Doctor David Owen**

Undiscovered Slough

A Trip Down Memory Lane, with the late **Sir Arthur Blunket** (rpt.).
A delightful journey through the nooks and crannies of Slough's mid-town supermarket complex, as Sir Arthur remembers, in discussion with **Michael Bentine, Bob Monkhouse** and **Steve Davis**, what it all was like before the Boer War when he used to live in Beaconsfield.
Music by **The Swingle Singers.**

Presented by **The late Sir Noel Edmonds Breakfast-Show**

Yes, it had to come: thank you letters are the very worst thing about Christmas, and we would like to thank you for buying this book by relieving you of the burden of the dullest of them.
Here then are your **Special Crisis Kit Ready To Post Thank You Letters to Granny** (providing she is, of course, still alive – see **Crisis Two: Kill Granny** and **Appendix Two: Eat Granny**).
Obviously there are some problems in making them realistic, but we hope we have foreseen most of them.

26th December

So excited by
Your present
I can't remember
Our Address.

Dear Granny,
What a wonderful Christmas it has been. Never have I been more excited by my presents. Dad gave me a typewriter, and then, believe it or not, Mum gave me a photocopier. This means that I can type out all my letters – see, I'm typing this one – and then, if I want to keep a copy, I can! In fact, I'm going to send you a slightly reduced copy of this one instead of the real letter, just so you'll believe I've actually got all this new equipment.

But enough of those great presents. Thank you, thank you, thank you for your wonderful presents. It was EXACTLY, I mean EXACTLY what I wanted. How did you know? People always say that grandmothers always give crummy presents; you know the sort of thing; but not my grandmother: no sirree! Photocopiers and typewriters are all very well, but what I really needed this year was a dishcloth featuring pictures of rare English birds. You see I have recently become very keen on drying up and this will really encourage my new hobby. And as for those rare English birds – well, they are so rare, aren't they, that it's a real shame not to be able to recognise them when they do pop up.

Well, I must stop now, as I want to get down and do the dishes before anyone else get to them – oops – using the present already! Lots of love and thanks again, Granny.

I love you, you know.
Your loving grandchild.

P.S. Perhaps some washing up liquid, all of my own, for my birthday – just a hint!

IF THIS IS NOT EXACTLY RIGHT USE THIS ONE

26th December

So excited by
Your present
I can't remember
Our Address.

Dear Granny,
What a wonderful Christmas it has been. Never have I been more excited by my presents. Dad gave me a typewriter, and then, believe it or not, Mum gave me a photocopier. This means that I can type out all my letters – see, I'm typing this one – and then, if I want to keep a copy, I can! In fact, I'm going to send you a slightly reduced copy of this one instead of the real letter, just so you'll believe I've actually got all this new equipment.

But enough of those great presents. Thank you, thank you, thank you for your fabulous present. It was EXACTLY, I mean EXACTLY what I wanted. HOW COULD YOU KNOW? People say that grandmothers always give crummy presents that you don't want. You know the sort of thing: dish cloths with pictures of rare English birds on them. But not you, no sirree.

Well, I must stop now. A friend has just come round and I want to show him your present straight away, since it is my favourite of all.

Thanks again, all my love,
Your loving grandchild.

P.S. Don't you love the formal signing off?!

Crisis Kit Appendix One:
What to say to Granny on the Telephone.
Grannies still don't trust these new-fangled electronic telephones, so the thing to do is to pretend that there is something wrong with the line. Keep repeating yourself, going silent for seconds and then yelling very loud. You should be off in seconds with a routine such as this: "Hullo Granny, Merry Ch – BARP! Sorry about that, there's something – BEEP-BEEP-Beep – Look, I better get off, get off the line before the phone (PAUSE) packs up completely up completely BARP! Lots of (LONG PAUSE) BARP! lovely Granny, lovely Granny, sorry, BARP! BARP! . . . ucking hell!

Crisis Kit Appendix Two:
When the Turkey burns and Your Mother Has a Nervous Breakdown. Fortunately, there is a swift and easy answer to this crisis:
Eat Granny: You will find that a Granny can be easily disguised as a turkey with a little bit of cunning basting and trussing. As for the taste, well, smothered as it will be by bread sauce, cranberry sauce and the taste of slightly off brussels sprouts, there is no chance that anyone will notice the difference.

HAVE A GOOD CHRISTMAS!

COMING TO TERMS WITH THE CHRISTMAS
MESSAGE REMAINED A CONSIDERABLE PROBLEM
FOR YOUNG BILLY...

ADRIAN MOLE'S CHRISTMAS

by Sue Townsend

CHRISTMAS EVE

Something dead strange has happened to Christmas. It's just not the same as it used to be when I was a kid. In fact I've never really got over the trauma of finding out that my parents had been lying to me annually about the existence of Santa Claus.

To me then at the age of 11, Santa Claus was a bit like God: all-seeing, all-knowing, but without the lousy things that God allows to happen: earthquakes, famines, motorway crashes. I would lie in bed under the blankets (how crude the word blankets sounds today when we are all conversant with the Tog rating of continental quilts), my heart pounding and my palms sweaty in anticipating of the virgin *Beano* album. I would imagine big jolly Santa looking from his celestial sledge over our cul-de-sac and saying to his elves: Give Adrian Mole something decent this year. He is a good lad. He never forgets to put the lavatory seat down. Ah . . . the folly of the child!

Alas, now at the age of maturity (16 years, four months and three days, five hours and six minutes) . . . I know that my parents walk around the town centre, wild-eyed with consumer panic, chanting desperately: "What shall we get for Adrian?" Is it any wonder that Christmas Eve has lost its awe?

2.15 am

Just got back from the Midnight Service. As usual it dragged on for far too long. My Mother started getting fidgety after the first hour of the Co-op Young Wives' carols. She kept whispering: "I shall have to go home soon or that bloody turkey will never be thawed out for the morning." Once again the Nativity playlet was ruined by having a live donkey in the church. It never behaves itself and always causes a major disturbance, so why does the vicar inflict it on us? OK, so his brother-in-law runs a donkey sanctuary, but so what? To be fair, the effect of the Midnight Service was dead moving. Even to me who is a committed nihilistic existentialist.

CHRISTMAS DAY

Not a bad collection of presents considering my Dad's redundant. I got the grey zip-up cardigan I asked for. My Mother said: "If you want to look like a 16-year-old Frank Bough then go ahead, wear the thing!" The Oxford Dictionary will come in useful for increasing my word power. But the best present of all was the electric shaver. I have already had three shaves. My chin is as smooth as a billiard ball. Someone should have got one for Leon Brittan. It's not good for Britain's image for a Cabinet Minister to go around looking as though he has been in the cells of a New York police station all night. The lousy Sugdens, my Mother's inbred Norfolk relations, turned up at 11.30am. So I got my parents out of bed and then retired to my room to read my *Beano* annual. Perhaps I am too worldly and literate nowadays but I was quite disappointed at its childish level of humour. I emerged from my bedroom in time for Christmas dinner and was forced to engage the Sugdens in conversation. They told me in minute mind-boggling detail about the life-cycle of King Edward potatoes, from tuber to chip pan. They were not a bit interested in my conversation about the Norwegian Leather Industry. In fact they looked bored. Just my luck to have Philistines for relations!

Dinner was late as usual, my Mother has never learnt the secret of coordinating the ingredients of a meal. Her gravy is always made before the roast potatoes have turned brown. I went into the kitchen to give her some advice, but she shouted "Get out of it" through the steam. When it came the meal was quite nice but there was no witty repartee over the table, not a single hilarious anecdote was told. In fact I wish I had my Xmas dinner with Ned Sherrin. His relations are dead lucky to have him. I bet their sides ache from laughing.

The Sugdens do not approve of drink, so every time my parents even *looked* at a bottle of spirits they tightened their lips and sipped at their tea. And it is possible to do both. (I have seen it with my own eyes.) In the evening we all had a desultory game of cards. Grandfather Sugden won £4,000 off my Father. There was a lot of joking about my Father giving Grandad Sugden an IOU, but my Father said to me in the kitchen: "No way am I putting my name to paper, that mean old git would have me in court as fast as you could say King Edward!"

The Sugdens went to bed early on our rusty camp beds. They were leaving for Norfolk at dawn because they were worried about potato poachers. I now know why my Mother turned out to be wilful and prone towards alcohol abuse, it is a reaction against her lousy moronic upbringing in the middle of the potato field.

BOXING DAY

I was awoken at dawn by the sound of Grandad Sugden's rusty Ford Escort refusing to start. I know I should have gone down into the street and helped to push it but Grandma Sugden seemed to be doing all right on her own. It must be all those years of flinging potato sacks about. My parents were wisely pretending to be asleep, but I know they were awake because I could hear coarse laughter coming from their bedroom, and when the Sugden's engine came alive and the Escort finally turned the corner of our cul-de-sac I distinctly heard the sound of a champagne cork popping and the chink of glasses. Not to mention the loud "Cheers".

Went back to sleep but the dog licked me awake at 9.30 so I took it for a walk past Pandora's house. Her dad's Volvo was not in the drive so they must be staying with their rich relations. On the way back I passed Barry Kent who was kicking a football up against the wall of the old people's home. He seemed full of seasonal goodwill for once, and I stopped to talk to him. He asked what I had had for Christmas. I told him and asked him what he had had. He looked embarrassed and said "I ain't 'ad much this year 'cos our Dad's lost his job." I asked him what happened and he said "I dunno, our Dad says Mrs Thatcher took it off him." I said: "What, personally?" Barry shrugged and said "Well that's what our Dad reckons."

Barry asked me back to his house for a cup of tea so I went to show that I bore him no grudges from the days when he used to demand money with menaces from me. The outside of the Kents' council house looked very grim (Barry told me that the council has been promising to mend the fences, doors and windows for years) but the inside looked magical. Paper chains were hung everywhere almost completely hiding the cracks in the walls and ceilings. Mr Kent had been out into the community and found a large branch, painted it with white gloss paint and stuck it into the empty paint tin. This branch very effectively took the place of a Christmas tree in my opinion, but Mrs Kent said sadly: "But it's not the same really, not if the only reason you've got it is because you can't afford to have a real plastic one." I was going to say that their improvised tree was modernistic and Hi Tech but I kept my mouth shut.

I asked the Kent children what they had had for Christmas and they said "Shoes", so I had to pretent to admire them. I had no choice because they kept sticking them under my nose. Mr and Mrs Kent laughed and said: "And Mr Kent and me gave each other a packet of fags!" As you know, dear diary, I disapprove of smoking but I could understand their need to have a bit of pleasure at Christmas. So I did not give them my anti-smoking lecture. I did not ask any more questions and politely declined the mince pies they offered . . . from where I was sitting I could see into their empty pantry.

Walking back home I wondered how my parents were able to buy decent Christmas presents for me. After all my Father and Mr Kent are both innocent victims of the robot culture where machines are preferred to people.

As I came through the back door I found out. My Father was saying: "But how the hell am I going to pay the next Access bill, Pauline?" My Mother said:"We'll have to sell something, George; whatever happens we've got to hang on to at least one credit card, because it's impossible to live on the dole and social security." So my family's Christmas prosperity is a thin veneer. We've had it on credit.

In the afternoon we went round to Grandma's for Boxing Day tea. As she slurped out the trifle she complained bitterly about her Christmas Day spent in the Evergreen Club. She said: "I knew I shouldn't have gone; that filthy communist Bert Baxter got disgustingly drunk on a box of liqueur chocolates and sang crude words at the carol service!" My Father said: "You should have come to us, Mum. I did ask you." Grandma said: "You only asked me *once* and anyway the Sugdens were there." This last remark offended my Mother. She is always criticising the family but she hates anybody else to do the same. The tea ended in disaster when I broke a plate that she had had for years. I know Grandma loves me but I have to record that on this occasion she looked at me with murder in her eyes.

She said: "Nobody will ever know what that plate meant to me." I offered to pick the pieces up but she pushed me away with the end of the hand brush. I went into the bathroom to cool down and after 20 minutes my Mother banged on the door and said: "C'mon, Adrian, we're going home, Grandma's just told your Dad that it's his own fault that he's been made redundant."

As I passed through the living room the silence between my Father and my Grandma was as solid as a double-glazed window. As we passed Pandora's house in the car I saw that the fairy lights in her garden were switched on, so I asked my parents to drop me off. Pandora was ecstatic to see me at first, she raved about the present I bought her (a solid gold bracelet from Tesco's, £2.49), but after a bit she cooled a bit and started going on about the Christmas house party she'd been to. She made a lot of references to a boy called Crispin Wartog-Lowndes. Apparently he is an expert rower and he rowed Pandora across a lake on Christmas Day. Whilst doing so he quoted from the works of Percy Bysshe Shelley. According to Pandora there was a mist on the lake. I got into silent jealous rage and imagined pushing Crispin Wartog-Lowndes's stupid face under the lake until he'd forgotten about Pandora, Christmas and Shelley. I got into bed as I am worn out with all the emotion. In fact as I lay in the dark, tears came to my eyes, especially when I remembered the Kents' empty pantry.

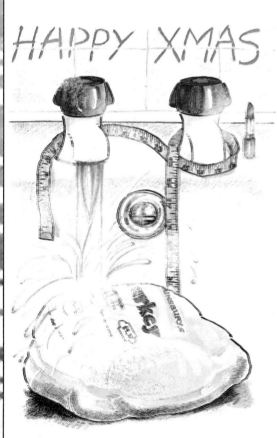

The Alternative Carol Sheet

Good King Wenceslas 2

The story so far.

"Good" King Wenceslas has looked out and seen a poor man struggling through the snow. He and a faithful page set out through a bitter storm to bring the pauper food and wine. At the end of part one, the page has almost died of cold, but been revived by the warmth of the King's goodness.

The moral of the tale has been firmly stated . . .

Therefore Christian men, be sure,
Wealth or rank possessing,
Ye who now do bless the poor
Shall yourselves find blehessing.

But, as often in a sequel, things don't turn out exactly the same as you might have expected . . .

1 Good King Wenceslas arrived
At the poor man's dwelling,
Cold and only half alive,
Feet and fingers swelling.
Brightly shone the fire inside,
Where the poor man rested,
With his daughter by his side,
Sweet and unmolested.

2 "My lord, your royal presence here,
It does not surprise me,
Look now carefully at my ear,
Do you recognise me?"
"O my God, it cannot be!"
"Yes, 'good' King it may be.
I am your sworn enemy,
You murdered my baby.

3 "So I hatched a cunning plan,
Devious and witty,
Bought myself some pauper's clothes
Made my hair all shitty.
I knew you'd come out in hope
You'd inspire a carol,
'stead of which, you stupid dope,
You're over a barrel."

4 "Not so fast," spake up the page,
Who had been most quiet,
"If you want to vent your rage,
Sir, I would not try it.
For I'm not a page at all,
But a noble knight, sir.
Brave Sir Roland is my name
I defend the right, sir."

5 Then he did his sword unlock
And made to kill the pauper,
But he found his way was blocked
By the pauper's daughter.
"Not so fast," the daughter said,
"Hold thy sword, Sir Roland —
I am not a girl at all,
But the King of Poland.

6 "This poor man he does not lie,
Wenceslas is nasty,
Baked his child into a pie,
And ate it like a pasty.
He pretends to be a saint
To get to heaven faster,
But the truth is that he ain't:
He's an utter bastard."

7 Hearing which the noble knight,
In anger was not lacking,
With a sword he killed the shite,
Sent Wenceslas packing.
Therefore hypocrites be sure,
Bet you more than thruppence,
If you make pies of the poor,
You'll get your comeuppance.

White Christmas

As we approach the twenty-seventh Christmas without snow, the words become increasingly ridiculous and frustrating. Here, for your delectation, are two alternative versions.

Grey Christmas

I'm dreaming of a Grey Christmas
Just like the ones we used to know,
Where the rain keeps falling,
And the weather is appalling,
And there's never hide nor hair of snow.

I'm dreaming of a Grey Christmas,
And that's exactly what I'll get.
If you live in Britain you can bet,
That all your Christmases will be wet.

The Holly and the Ivy

The thing wrong with this carol is that they only mention the Ivy in order then cruelly and callously to say it is not as good as the Holly. Anyone with any interest in a fair and just society, the sort of thing Jesus was born and died for, should refuse to sing this hideous carol. If you must, we suggest you sing this short revised version.

The Holly and the Ivy,
When they are both full grown,
Of all the trees that are in the wood,
The Holly bears the Crown,
But the Ivy's very nice as well.

*It doesn't make sense rhythmically,
but it's sure as hell a lot more FAIR.*

Brown Christmas

I'm dreaming of a Brown Christmas,
Just like the ones we used to know,
Where tempers flicker,
And parents bicker,
And children's presents never go.

I'm dreaming of a Brown Christmas,
With the television never off,
It's the same from commoner to toff,
At Christmas, everyone's browned off.

'Willie is the root of all evil.'

Old Australian saying

Right now the world is in a dreadful state what with terrorists, famine and wheel clamping.

The cause of all these hideous scourges can be traced back to one source. A small but horribly formed individual, name of Willie.

A few weeks after God had finished making heaven and earth and had

They can't possibly mean me...

Hope this weather lasts for the weekend.

moved on to more important things Adam was doing a spot of weeding in the Garden of Eden. He was a really nice chap, sensitive, highly intelligent and in no way in need of a shrink.

He got on well with all the other animals, even the snakes, and they would always greet him with a big smile. One of the reasons for the big smile was that although he didn't know it, Adam didn't have a Willie.

Of course, this situation was too innocent to last. Adam began to feel something was missing, so he put in a 'person to deity' call to God.

Adam told God that he loved the animals and the pretty shrubs and that he wasn't really complaining.
"I just feel a bit lonely" he said.
"I know how you feel", said God. "I'm surrounded by angels and if anything they're even more boring than shrubs. I'll send you something to play with. It's called Willie and they say it's good for a lot of laughs. But from here on in, nothing is for nothing, so it'll cost you".

"I have no money", said Adam. "What will I pay you with?"

"Half your brain", said God.

Make up your mind-If you don't want it maybe Eve would like it...

That's salesmanship!

So Adam woke next morning with a Willie, and half his brain missing. Even so, he was still fairly bright, if a touch uncouth and aggressive suddenly.

Sadly, as we now know, this condition turned out to be hereditary, since God also sent Adam a nice girl called Nancy. (Adam nicknamed her Eve because he thought Nancy was a dumb name for the First Lady.)

She cost Adam a rib. Had he stumped up an arm and a leg though, he could have had a truly wondrous creature with four tits and French knickers, who didn't know the meaning of the word headache.

However, Nancy had a nice nature and, of course, an entire brain.

Anyway, Willie managed to get them evicted from Eden by making God mad at him for doing his snake and apple impression once too often.

And that was just the start. Over the next zillion years Willie had mankind firmly by the goolies. Fighting and fucking was the name of the game, not to mention office harassment.

Soon there were far too many people for the world to cope with. But they weren't all half-wits. Some had evolved a whole brain.

On the other hand some wound up with no brain at all, and were so irrational they even had Willie worried.

Those with no brain at all usually found themselves sucked into politics, often taking over entire countries. And the ones who missed out on countries protested by doing the same thing with airliners.

And there was the poor world wilting from Willie tyranny and sagging under the weight of all the people he had caused.

Luckily, the Angel Gabe noticed what was going on and gave God a nudge on the elbow.

"Jesus H. Christ," said God. "Will you be lookin at all them people! That Willie's certainly been busy." God hadn't been giving Earth his undivided attention what with the Universe to run. He'd assumed that earthquakes, floods, junk food and accidents in the home would keep the people level reasonable.

"Better nuke 'em", he said.

"Dunno about that," said Gabe. "A holocaust is a bit over the top. What about Pestilence?"

"Pestilence is doing the AIDS gig on the West Coast", said God. "But Famine seems to be at a loose end."

So God sent in Famine. To Africa.

"Why Africa?" asked Gabe. "You could get accused of you know what."

"I picked it with a pin", said God, eyes wide with innocence. "It could just as easily have been India."

But God's Will ain't what it used to be, and the Famine hit trouble.

A hairy musician with a whole brain, but no band, decided that famine was a very bad idea.

In hardly any time at all the saintly lad had organised huge gigs all over the world — music, sport, you name it. And vast amounts of money came flooding in to stop the famine. God was extremely pissed off.

"Who does this guy think he is? How can I run infinite space if people from a hick planet start messing up my plans?" God wasn't used to having his plans messed up.

"A cosmic view isn't easy when you're starving", said Gabe. "Besides, it was your idea to give the silly buggers free will".

"Well I'll nuke 'em then", said God crossly. "Should have done that in the first place".

"Better find a scapegoat though", said Gabe. "Who do we know with a Polo Mint for a brain?"

Gabe and God pondered hard for about a millionth of a second before coming up with the ideal candidate...

Crudeword Crossword
(A very hard one)

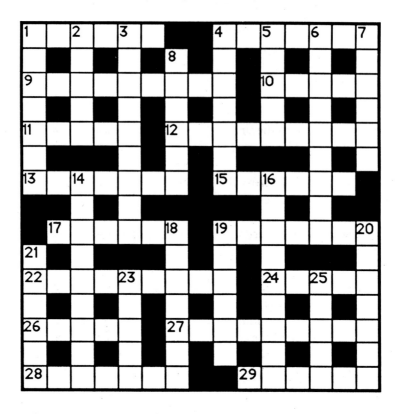

Across

1 Smell bone in cat's bum (6)
4 A lot of 1 and French sex (7)
9 Object to mother losing her first whatsit (9)
10 Does number 2's game (5)
11 *The Magic Flute* for example? A rope trick (5)
12 Superheat problems? Some put the thermometer here (2, 3, 4)
13 Get this to bugger off (7)
15 I am in bed with America, love-making (6)
17 Oval trophy (3-3)
19 Lassie and Joan Collins snaffle church Latin art (7)
22 This tunnel is not yours to shag (9)
24 Okay, screw him (5)
26 Two times two thirds of two diamonds (5)
27 Shit, you sound inclined to be drunk (9)
28 Elite newspaperman came (7)
29 Master wrong for academic channel (6)

Down

1 Ham up over-acting in deer-skin (7)
2 What lines a stomach? Crap. (5)
3 It's a corgi going wild enjoying group sex (9)
4 Strange, like this puzzle (7)
5 Soho employer is unclean, without an article on (5)
6 Foul drama, dirty (4, 5)
7 Balls up games, 26 (6)
8 Steeped in Drambuie, 'e gets pissed. No artist (6)
14 Penis duct can make wonderful music (5, 4)
16 15 — with us is an unfinished 24 (9)
18 Cavorted around with crap out wrong end? (7)
19 But Robin isn't his military master (6)
20 Nuts in here, funny custom. Right! (7)
21 Some have me tickled — it makes you want to throw up (6)
23 Millions tailed in search for 17's first half (5)
25 Anserine creatures see up both ends of Girl Guide (5)

Answers not on page 69

The Private Life Of Genghis Khan

by Douglas Adams

(based on an original sketch
by Douglas Adams and Graham Chapman)

The last of the horsemen disappeared into the smoke and the thudding of their hooves receded into the grey distance.

The smoke hung on the land. It drifted across the setting sun, which lay like an open wound across the western sky.

In the ringing silence that followed the battle, very, very few, pitifully few cries could be heard from the bloody, mangled wreckage on the fields.

Ghostlike figures, stunned with horror, emerged from the woods, stumbled and then ran forward crying — women, searching for their husbands, brothers, fathers, lovers first amongst the dying and then amongst the dead. The flickering light by which they searched was that of their burning village, which had that afternoon officially become part of the Mongol Empire.

The Mongols.

From out of the wastes of central Asia they had swept, a savage force for which the world was utterly unprepared. They swept like a wildly wielded scythe, hacking, slashing, obliterating all that lay in their path, and calling it conquest.

And throughout the lands that feared them now or would come to fear them, no name inspired more terror than that of their leader, Genghis Khan: the greatest of the Asian warlords, he stood alone, revered as a god among warriors, marked out by the cold light of his grey-green eyes, the savage furrow of his brow, and the fact that he could beat the shit out of any of them.

Later that night the moon rose, and by its light a small party of horsemen carrying torches rode quietly out from the Mongol encampment that sprawled over nearby hills. A casual observer would not have noticed anything remarkable about the man who rode at their centre, muffled in a heavy cloak, tense, hunched forward on his horse as if weighed down by a heavy burden, because a casual observer would have been dead.

The band rode a few miles through the moonlit woods, picking their way along the paths until they came at last to a small clearing, and here they reined their horses in and waited on their leader.

He moved his horse slowly forward and surveyed the small group of peasant huts that stood huddled together in the centre of the clearing trying very hard at short notice to look deserted.

Hardly any smoke at all was rising from the primitive chimney stacks. Virtually no light appeared at the windows, and not a sound could be heard from any of them save that of a small child saying "Shhhhh . . ."

For a moment a strange green fire seemed to flash from the eyes of the Mongol leader. A heavy deadly kind of thing that you could hardly call a smile drew itself through his fine wispy beard. The strange kind of smiley thing would signify (briefly) to anyone who was stupid enough to look that there was nothing a Mongol warlord liked better after a day hacking people to bits than a big night out.

The door flew open. A Mongol warrior surged into the hut like a savage wind. Two children ran screaming to their mother who was cowering wide-eyed in the corner of the tiny room. A dog yelped.

The warrior hurled his torch on to the still glowing fire, and then threw the dog on to it. That would teach it to be a dog. The last surviving man of the family, a grey and aged grandfather, stepped bravely forward, eyes flashing. With a flash of his sword the Mongol whipped off the old man's head which trundled across the floor and fetched up leaning rakishly against a table leg. The old man's body stood tensely for a moment, not knowing what to think. As it began slowly, majestically to topple forward, Khan strode in and pushed it brusquely aside. He surveyed the happy domestic scene and bestowed a grim kind of smile on it. Then he walked over to a large chair and sat in it, testing it first for comfort. When he was satisfied with it he heaved a heavy sigh and sat back in front of the fire on which the dog was now blazing merrily.

The warrior grabbed at the terrified woman, pushed her children roughly aside and brought her, trembling, in front of the mighty Khan.

She was young and pretty, with long bedraggled black hair. Her bosom heaved and her face was stark with fright.

Khan regarded her with a slow contemptuous look.

"Does she know," he said at length in a low, dead voice, 'who I am?"

"You . . . you are the mighty Khan!" cried the woman.

Khan's eyes fixed themselves on hers.

"Does she know," he hissed, "what I want of her?"

"I . . . I'll do anything for you, O Khan," stammered the woman, "but spare my children!"

Khan said quietly, "Then begin." His eyes dropped and he gazed distantly into the fire.

Nervously shaking with fear the woman stepped forward and laid a tentative pale hand on Khan's arm.

The soldier smacked her hand away.

"Not that!" he barked.

The woman started back, aflutter. She realised she would have to do better. Still shaking, she knelt down on the floor and started gently to push apart the Khan's knees.

"Stop that!" roared the soldier and shoved her violently backwards. Bewilderment began to mix with the terror in her eyes as she cowered on the floor.

"Come on," snapped the soldier, "ask him what kind of day he's had."

"What . . .?" she wailed. "I don't . . . I don't understand what . .'"

The soldier seized her, span her into a half nelson, and jabbed the point of his sword against her throat.

"I said ask him," he hissed, "what kind of day he's had!"

The woman gasped with pain and incomprehension. The sword jabbed again.

"Say it!"

"Er, what sort . . . of . . . er, day . .'" she said in a hesitant, strangled squeak, "have you . . . had?"

"Dear!" hissed the soldier. "Say dear!"

Her eyes bulged in horror at the sword.

"What sort of day have you had . . . dear?" she asked querulously.

Khan looked up briefly, wearily.

"Oh, same as usual," he said. "Violent."

He gazed back at the fire again.

"Right," said the soldier to the woman, "go on."

She relaxed very slightly. She seemed to have passed some kind of test. Perhaps it would be straightforward from now on and she could at least get it over with. She moved nervously forward and started to caress the Khan again.

The soldier hurled her savagely across the room, kicked her and yanked her screaming to her feet again.

"I said stop that!" he bellowed. He pulled her face close to his and breathed a lungful of cheap wine and week-old rancid goat-fat fumes at her, which failed to cheer her up because it reminded her sharply of her late lamented husband who used to do the same thing to her every night. She sobbed.

"Be nice to him!" the Mongol snarled and spat one of his unwanted teeth at her. "Ask him how his work's going!"

She gawped at him. The nightmare was continuing. A stinging blow landed on her cheek.

"Just say to him," the soldier snarled again, "'How's the work going, dear?'" He shoved her forward.

"How . . . how's the work going . . . dear?" she yelped miserably.

The soldier shook her. "Put some affection into it!" he roared.

She sobbed again. "How . . . how's the work going . . . dear?" she yelped miserably again, but this time with a kind of pathetic pout at the end.

The mighty Khan sighed.

"Oh, not too bad I suppose," he said in a world-weary tone. "We swept through Manchuria a bit and spilt a lot of blood there. That was in the morning, then this afternoon was mainly pillaging, though there was a bit of bloodshed around half four. What sort of day have you had?"

So saying, he pulled a couple of scroll maps from out of his furs and started to study them abstractedly by the light of the smouldering dog.

The Mongol warrior pulled a glowing poker out of the fire and advanced menacingly on the woman.

"Tell him! Go on!"

She leapt back with a shriek.

Tell him!

"Er, my husband and father were killed!" she said.

"Oh yes dear?" said Khan absently, not looking up from his maps.

"Dog was burnt!"

"Oh, er, really?"

"Well, er, that's about it, really . . . er . . ?"

The soldier advanced on her with the poker again.

"Oh, and I was tortured a bit!" shrieked the woman.

Khan looked up at her. "What?" he said, vaguely. "Sorry dear, I was just reading this . . ?"

"Right," said the soldier, "nag him!"

"What?"

"Just say, 'Look Genghis, put that thing away while I'm talking to you. Here I am, spend all day slaving over a hot . . .'"

"He'll *kill* me!"

"Bleeding kill you if you don't."

"I can't stand it!" cried the woman and collapsed on the floor. She flung herself on the great Khan's feet. "Don't torment me," she wailed. "If you mean to rape me, then rape me, but don't . . ?"

The great Khan surged to his feet and glowered down at her. "No," he muttered savagely, "you'd only laugh — you're just like all the others."

He stormed out of the hut and rode off into the night in such a rage that he almost forgot to burn down the village before he left.

After another particularly vicious day the last of the horsemen disappeared into the smoke and the thudding of their hooves receded into the grey distance.

The smoke hung on the land. It drifted across the setting sun, which lay like an open wound across the western sky.

In the ringing silence that followed the battle, very, very few, pitifully few cries could be heard from the bloody, mangled wreckage on the fields.

Ghostlike figures, stunned with horror, emerged from the woods, stumbled and then ran forward crying — women, searching for their husbands, brothers, fathers, lovers first amongst the dying and then amongst the dead.

Far away behind the screen of smoke thousands of horsemen arrived at their sprawling camp, and with a huge amount of clatter, shouting and comparing of backhand slashes they dismounted and instantly started in on the cheap wine and rancid goat fat.

In front of his splendidly bedraped Imperial tent a bloodstained and battle-weary Khan dismounted.

"Which battle was that?" he asked his son, Ogdai, who had ridden with him. Ogdai was a young and ambitious general, keenly interested in viciousness of all kinds. He was hoping to improve on his own known world record for the highest number of peasants impaled on a single sword thrust and would be getting in some practice that night.

He strode up to his father.

"It was the Battle of Samarkand, O Khan!" he proclaimed, and rattled his sword in a tremendously impressive way.

Khan folded his arms and leant on his horse, looking over it across the dreadful mess they'd made of the valley beneath them.

"Oh, I can't tell the difference any more," he said with a sigh. "Did we win?"

"Oh yes! Yes! Yes!" exclaimed Ogdai with fierce pride. "It was a mighty victory indeed! Indeed it was!" he added and waggled his sword again. He drew it excitedly and made a few practice thrusts. Yes, he thought to himself, tonight he was going to go for the six.

Khan screwed his face up at the gathering dusk.

"Oh dear," he said, "after twenty years of these two-hour battles I get the feeling that there must be more to life, you know." He turned, lifted up the front of his torn and bloodied gold embroidered tunic and stared down at his own hairy tummy. "Here, feel this," he said, "do you think I'm putting it on a bit?"

Ogdai gazed at the great Khan's tummy with a mixture of awe and impatience.

"Er no," he said. "No, not at all." With a flick of his fingers Ogdai summoned a servant to bring the maps to him, ran him through, and as he fell caught from his nerveless but not entirely surprised fingers the plans of the grand campaign.

"Now, O Khan," he said, spreading the map over the back of another servant who stood specially hunched over for the purpose, "we must push forward to Persia, and then we shall be poised to take over the whole world!"

"No, look, feel that," said Khan, pinching a fold of skin between his fingers, "do you think . . ?"

"Khan!" interrupted Ogdai urgently, "we are on the point of conquering the *world!*" He stabbed at the map with a knife, catching the servant beneath a nasty nick on

113

his left lung.

"When?" said Khan with a frown.

Ogdai threw up his arms in exasperation. "Tomorrow!" he said. "We start tomorrow!"

"Ah, well, tomorrow's a bit difficult, you see," said Khan. He puffed out his cheeks and thought for a moment. "The thing is that next week I've got this lecture on carnage techniques in Bokhara, and I thought I'd use tomorrow to prepare it."

Ogdai stared at him in astonishment as the map-bearing servant slowly collapsed on his foot.

"Well, can't you put that off?" he exclaimed.

"Well, you see, they've paid me quite a lot of money for it already, so I'm a bit committed."

"Well, *Wednesday?*"

Khan pulled a scroll from out of his tunic and looked through it, shaking his head slowly. "Not sure about Wednesday . . ."

"*Thursday?*"

"No, Thursday I am certain about. We've got Ogdai and his wife coming round to dinner, and I'd kind of promised . . ."

"But I *am* Ogdai!"

"Well, there you are then. You wouldn't be able to make it either."

Ogdai's silence was only disturbed by the sound of thousands of hairy Mongols shouting and fighting and getting pissed.

"Look," he said quietly, "will you be ready to conquer the world . . . on Friday?"

Khan sighed.

"Well, the secretary comes in on Friday mornings."

"Does she?"

"All those letters to answer. You'd be astonished at the demands people try to make on my time you know." He slouched moodily against his horse. "Would I sign this, would I appear there. Would I please do a sponsored massacre for charity. So that usually takes till at least three, then I had hoped to get away early for a long weekend. Now Monday, Monday . . ."

He consulted his scroll again.

"Monday's out, I'm afraid. Rest and recuperation, that's one thing I do insist upon. Now how about Tuesday?"

The strange keening noise that could be heard in the distance at this moment sounded like the normal everyday wailing of women and children over their slaughtered menfolk and Khan paid no mind to it. A light bobbed on the horizon.

"Tuesday — look, I'm free in the morning — no, hold on a moment, I'd sort of made a date for meeting this awfully interesting chap who knows absolutely everything about under*stand*ing things, which is something I'm awfully bad at. Now that's a pity because that was my only free day next week. Now, *next* Tuesday we could usefully think about — or is that the day I . . ."

The keening sound continued, in fact it grew, but it was so lightly borne upon the evening breeze that it still did not intrude upon Khan's senses. The approaching light was so pale as to be indistinguishable from that of the moon, which was bright that night.

". . . so that's more or less the whole of March out," said Khan, "I'm afraid."

"April?" asked Ogdai, wearily. He idly whipped out a passing peasant's liver, but the joy had gone out of it. He flipped the thing listlessly off into the dark. A dog which had grown very fat over the years by the simple expedient of staying close to Ogdai at all times leapt on it. These were not pleasant times.

"Well, no, April's out," said Khan "I'm going to Africa in April, that's one thing I had promised myself."

The light approaching them through the night sky had now at last attracted the attention of one or two other leading Mongols in the vicinity, who, wonderingly, stopped hitting each other and stabbing things and drew near.

"Look," said Ogdai, himself still unaware of what things were coming to pass, "can we please agree that we will conquer the world in May, then?"

The mighty Khan sucked doubtfully on his teeth.

"Well, I don't like to commit myself that far in advance. One feels so tied down if one's life is completely mapped out beforehand. I should be doing more reading, for heaven's sake—when am I going to find time for that? Anyway —" he sighed and scratched at his scroll, " 'May — possible conquest of the world'. Now I've only pencilled that in, so don't regard it as absolutely definite — but keep on at me about it and we'll see how it goes. Hello, what's that?"

Slowly, with the grace of a beautiful woman stepping into a bath, a long slim silver craft lowered itself gently to the ground. Soft light streamed from it. From its opening doorway stepped a tall elegant creature with a curiously fine grey-green complexion. It walked slowly towards them.

In its path lay the dark figure of a peasant who had been crying quietly to himself since he had watched his liver being eaten by Ogdai's dog and had known that no way was he going to get it back, and wondered how on earth his poor wife was going to cope now. He chose this moment finally to pass on to better things.

The tall alien stepped over him with distaste and, though you would have had to read his face very closely to realise this, a little envy. He nodded briefly to each of the gathered Mongol leaders in turn, and pulled a small clipboard out from under his heavy metallic robe.

"Good evening," it said in a small weaselly voice, "my name is Wowbagger, also called the Infinitely Prolonged, I shall not trouble you with the reasons why. Greetings."

He turned and addressed the completely pop-eyed mighty Khan.

"You are Genghis Khan? Genghis Temüjin Khan, son of Yesügei?"

The diary scrolls slipped from Khan's hands to the ground. The pale luminescence from Wowbagger's ship suffused his wondering, ravaged, careworn yellow features. As in a dream the mighty Emperor stepped forward in acknowledgement.

"Can I just check the spelling?" said the alien, showing him the clipboard, "I would hate to get it wrong at this stage and then have to start all over again, I really would."

Khan nodded faintly.

"Right number of aitches, then?" said the alien.

Again, the transfigured Emperor slightly inclined his face, while his eyes still boggled.

"Good," said Wowbagger, and made a little tick on his clipboard. He looked up. "Genghis Khan," he said, "you are a wanker; you are a tosspot; you are a very tiny piece of turd. Thank you." With that he retreated into his ship and flew off.

There was a nasty kind of silence.

Later that year Genghis Khan stormed into Europe in such a rage that he almost forgot to burn down Asia before he left.

Don't Children Say The Darndedest Things!!!!

Dear Santa,
My name is Jememy and i hope
that you are vary well. My mummy
Says that you Live in Iceland and
that it is vary cold there. My frend
Alexanda franks Says you dont Live
in Iceland becose you dont Live
anywhere becose you dont exist, but
he smells and is a Lya and
thinks hes terable clever and
Shows off could you please bring me
a bysacal at Christmas. I know
that my stockin is not big enuff but
If you Just put the handle bars
in the stockin. I promise not to guess
What it is until I open it.

I Love you
Jermey

Dear Santa,
My name is Alice and I am
5 and I want some dolls
for Chrissmas. How old are you?

I think you must bee very old
becos you have a beerd
I don't have a beerd.

Alice Myerson
Aged 5.

P.S. If I were you I woodnt give any
prezents to alexzander Franks. I
won't tell yoo why becoss I'm not
a sneek.

Deer Santa

Christmas time is here again, time to think about the lovely baby Jesus popping out of the lovely Mary, who was very mild. Did you bring the little baby Jesus presents as well? I hope so.

Alexander Franks who thinks he is so clever, said to me that you dont exist and that ~~in fact~~ you are in fact my Dad and my Mum. I told him that they were lying cos my Dad hasnt got a red nose and you hav.

George Kotter,

---

ere Santer,

Police give me sum Akshun man and fings. I hope you are not my Mum and Dad like Alexandre says, cos I dont like them and I lov yu.

Peter Smith.

Dear Santa,

This year I came second in my class with 72 percent. My Mum and Dad said if I did well, Santa would bring me lots of presents. I hope they passed the message on to you !!! (Those are exclamation marks: we have just learned how to use them) Top in the class was Alexander francs with 99%, but he cant be that clever because he says you are my Mum and Dad.

Love Charles Copeland.

P.S. I am writing in ink now as you can see. I was the second in the class to write in ink.

118

Dear Mum & Dad,

Homework tonight is a "Letter to Santa" for some charity compilation,
(overpriced,intro by Nanette Newman,smudged drawing of a Santa with
three arms on the front,you know the kind of caper)so I thought I'd
just drop you a line about the Christmas night arrangements.

1/I think we should go on with the traditional set-up for Granny's sake.
I hope you agree with that,although I know it does mean a little extra
shopping:but you know,any kind of garbage,I don't mind,and she won't
notice.

2/Delivery time should I think be left flexible:I'm likely to be
watching video late,so perhaps we could have some kind of signal. You
knock twice,I'll pop the vid on pause,switch off the lights,you come in,
dump the gear,and then I'll get on with the tape and 'promise not to
look' (isn't it weird how one holds on to these primal traditions).

3/Could you please wake me up early,so I can check out the presents
before you get up,work out what I'm going to say about them. Again,it's
really for the sake of Gran,even though I suspect (another interesting
thing,the whole genetic question of how he stayed so gullible,and I got,
well,I don't like to use the word cynical,let's say,enlightened on
things) —and kind of depends on me for the sense of occasion.

4/Afterwards,if there's any of the gifts you want to fill out embarrass-
ing gaps with neighbours,kids and things like that,of course,don't fail
to ask. I'm sure we can come to some kind of arrangement,and I know how
these thihgs do go wrong,year after year —"plus ca change,plus c'est la
meme",eh?

    Anyway,better get on with the rest of the homework. Essay title,
"Write 100 words about the little baby Jesus" —interesting I think—
I'm going to do it about the myth of the boy child in mid-eastern
culture—depending on time I may get to the Norse God legends,but I'm
increasingly wondering whether they're relevant,or whether it isn't to
Islam I should be looking on the comparative religion questions.
Whatever,one way or way or the other it's up to scratch.

Check you out later,

Your loving son,

Al.

p.s. Can I sleep in again with you tonight? Saw the mouse monster aga
yesterday,unfortunately.

Your Favourite Christmas Hits!!!!!!!!!

**From K-Tel, for only $4.99
499 of Your Favourite
Christmas Hits!!!!!!!!!**

Including . . .
White Christmas — **Bing Crosby**
Blue Christmas — **Shakin' Stevens**
Purple Christmas — **Prince**
It's Going to be Lonely This Christmas — **Mud**
It's Going to be Christmas This Christmas — **Some Mistake Surely**
I Believe in Father Christmas — **Keith Emerson**
No You Don't — **Greg Lake**
All Right, I Don't Believe in Father Christmas Then — **Greg Lake**
I Saw Mommy Kissing Santa Claus — **The Ronettes**
At Least I Think They were Kissing — **The Ronettes**
It's Going to be Lonely This Christmas — **Andrew Ridgeley**
Tough Luck — You Should Have Asked for a Guitar Ten Christmases Ago,
Then I Mightn't Have Sacked You — **George Michael**
Like a Virgin — **Madonna**
"Like" being the Operative Word — **Sean Penn**
They Might Have been Having It Off, I Suppose — **The Ronettes**
When a Child is Born — **Johnny Mathis**
What Do You Know about Childbirth — You're A . . . — **Everybody**
Ah — Ah — Mustn't Say Anything Nasty — After All It is Christmas,
You Know — **The Dollis Hill Kindergarten Choir**

**AND MANY, MANY MORE SINGALONG SONGS
ON A GREAT ALBUM THAT YOU'LL
ON 26 DECEMBER
PROFOUNDLY REGRET YOU BOUGHT!!!**

The Official Supplement to The Meaning of Liff

John Lloyd and Douglas Adams
with
Stephen Fry

In Life, there are many hundreds of common experiences, feelings, situations and even objects which we all know and recognise, but for which no words exist.

On the other hand, the world is littered with thousands of spare words which spend their time doing nothing but loafing about on signposts pointing at places.

Our job, as John and I saw it in the original **Meaning of Liff**, was to get these words down off the signposts and into the mouths of babes and sucklings and so on, where they could start earning their keep in everyday conversation and making a more positive contribution to society.

However, since **The Meaning of Liff** was first published in 1984 it has become clear that there were some serious omissions in it, or rather not in it if you see what I mean. This supplement has been prepared in order to correct the situation. It has therefore no omissions in it, or rather it has the omissions from the original book in it, but in unomitted form. In other words the omissions have been omitted. It is possible, however, that this introduction will be left out and I won't be at all offended if it is.

Douglas Adams

ADDIS ABABA (n.)
The torrent of incomprehensible gibberish which emanates from the loudspeakers on top of cars covered in stickers.

AMPUS (n.)
A lurid bruise which you can't remember getting.

ANCRUM (n.)
Gormless petty-minded idiot, weedy-voiced bureaucrat, fool, nerd, employee of British Telecom.

BALZAN (n.)
The noise of a dustbin lid coming off in the middle of the night.

BELDING (n.)
The technical name for a stallion after its first ball has been cut off. Any field displaying the legend "Beware of the belding" should be taken extremely seriously.

BEPTON (n.)
One who beams benignly after burping.

BICKERSTAFF (n.)
The person in an office that everyone winges about in the pub. Many large corporations deliberately employ bickerstaffs in each department. For example, Sir Robert Maxwell is both Chairman and Chief Bickerstaff of Mirror Group Newspapers.

BLANDFORD FORUM (n.)
Any Radio 4 chat show.

BOTSWANA (n.)
Something which is more fruitfully used for a purpose other than that for which it was designed. A fishknife used to lever open a stubborn tin of emulsion is a fine example of botswana.

BOTTISHAM (n.)
The feeling you get which begins as an itch and gradually becomes an uncomfortable pain as you walk around after having been forced to wipe yourself with crispy lavatory paper.

BRUGES (pl. n.)
The hairs which collect in the mouth immediately

on commencing sex.

BURSLEM (n.)
One who goes on talking at 3 o'clock in the morning after everyone else has gone to sleep. The main institution to which burslems are confined is Radio 2.

CAIRO (vb.)
To make the noise of a spinning hubcap coming to rest.

COWCADDENS (n.)
A set of twelve cowcaddens makes an ideal and completely baffling wedding gift.

CRIEFF (vb.)
To agree sycophantically with a taxi-driver about immigration.

CRUDGINGTON (n.)
The dull heartache that descends on you when you realise that your parents actually intend to watch *Panorama* when there's something much more interesting just starting on the other side.

DUNSTER (n.)
A small child hired to bounce at dawn on the occupants of the spare bedroom in order to save on tea and alarm clocks.

DURSLEY (n.)
The Henry Cooper accent everyone puts on when they want to mimic a stupid person.

FAMAGUSTA (n.)
The draught which whistles between two bottoms that refuse to touch.

FISHTOFT (n.)
That which wives get fed up with removing from the pockets of husbands who work at Billingsgate.

FREMANTLE (vb.)
To steal things not worth the bother of stealing. One steals cars, money and silver. Book matches, airline eye-patches and individual pots of Trust House Forte apricot jam are merely fremantled.

FRITHAM (n.)
A paragraph that you get stuck on in a book. The more often you read it through the less it means to you.

FUSCHL (vb.)
To stare deliberately at each passenger in the tube carriage in turn, so that the person whose eye you accidentally caught to begin with won't think that you were only staring at them.

GAMMERSGILL (n.)
Embarrassed stammer you emit when a voice answers the phone and you realise that you haven't the faintest recollection of who it is you've just rung.

GARSTANG (n.)
The shock of seeing that there is someone still in lavatory after all when you emerge after a protracted rossetting (qv) session.

GARTLY STATION (n.)
Somewhere to stand getting cross because the person you're supposed to be meeting hasn't turned up and it's already twenty past one.

GARTNESS (n.)
The ability to say "No, no there's absolutely nothing the matter, what could possibly be the matter? And anyway I don't want to discuss it," without moving your lips.

GARVOCK (n.)
The action of putting your finger in your cheek and flicking it out with a "pock" noise.

GHENT (adj.)
Descriptive of the mood indicated by cartoonists by drawing a character's mouth as wavy line.

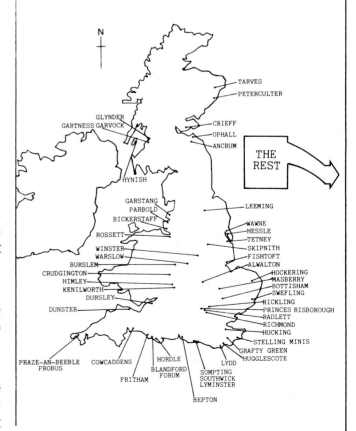

GLUD (n.)
The pinkish mulch found in the bottom of a lady's handbag.

GRAFTY GREEN (n.)
Money earned by Nigel Rees by copying down things that other people have said.

HESSLE (vb.)
To try and sort out which sleeve of a sweater is inside out when you're already halfway through putting it on.

HIMLEY (n.)
A Nazi war criminal who has somehow contrived to retire and grow vegetable marrows in the Cotswolds.

HOCKERING (pt. vb.)
Shouting at your wife because your boss shouted at you because his wife shouted at him.

HORDLE (vb.)
To dissemble in a fruity manner, like Donald Sinden.

HUCKING (pt. vb.)
Shouting at your husband because your boss shouted at you because her husband shouted at her.

HUGGLESCOTE (n.)
Someone who keenly opens a letter which says "You may already have won £10,000" on the outside.

HYNISH (adj.)
Descriptive of the state of mind in which you might as well give up trying to do whatever it is you're trying to do because you'll only muck it up.

JOPLIN (n.)
The material from which all clothes in Woolworths are made.

KANDAHAR (n.)
A short car chase in which the driver in front attempts to escape from the rude bastard who is hooting from behind. You drive faster and faster flicking v-signs in the mirror and cursing, until you get caught at the lights and the other driver gets out and taps at your window to say that your boot is open.

KENILWORTH (n.)
A measure. Defined as the proportion of the menu which the waiter speaks aloud that you can actually remember.

LEEMING (n.)
The business of making silly faces at babies.

LIMASSOL (n.)
The correct name for one of those little paper umbrellas which come in cocktails with too much pineapple juice in them.

LYDD (n.)
A lid. A lydd differs from a lid in that it has nothing to be a lid of, is at least 18 months old, and is sold in Ye Antique Shoppes.

LYMINSTER (n.)
A homosexual vicar.

MASBERRY (n.)
The sap of a giant Nigerian tree from which all canteen jams are made.

MANITOBA (n.)
A re-courtship ritual. The tentative and reluctant touching of spouses' toes in bed after an argument.

MEIKLE FLOAT (n.)
A sort of milk shake sold in health food shops. It is full of wheatgerm, yoghurt and bran and is even more impossible to drink than one of those tubs of cold sludge you get from McDonalds.

NOKOMIS (n.)
One who dresses like an ethnic minority to which they do not belong.

NOME (sfx.)
Latin suffix meaning: question expecting the answer "Oh really? How interesting."

PARAMATTA (n.)
The strange invisible substance into which car keys and spectacles mysteriously transmute when you put them down for a single second. They remain in this state for exactly the length of time it takes you to lose your temper, after which they mysteriously reappear as if nothing had happened.

PARBOLD (adj.)
Nearly brave enough to dive into a cold swimm-

ing pool on a windy day.

PETERCULTER (n.)
Someone you don't want to be friends with who rings you up at eight-monthly intervals and suggests you get together soon.

PLUVIGNER (n.)
The miniscule hole in the side of a biro.

POCKING (n.)
The pointless tapping of a cigarette before getting on with the business of smoking it.

PODEBRADY (n.)
The man in dirty white overalls hired to wander whistling round the corridors of a large corporation to make it look as if the management's getting something done.

POLLATOMISH (adj.)
Peevish, restless, inclined to pull the stuffing out of sofas.

PRAGUE (vb.)
To declaim loudly and pompously upon any subject about which one has less knowledge than at least one other person at the same table.

PRAZE-AN-BEEBLE (n.)
The self-congratulatory conversational style of guests on a Blandford forum (qv).

PRINCES RISBOROUGH (n.)
The right of any member of the Royal family to have people laugh at their jokey remarks, however weedy or pathetic.

PROBUS (n.)
The sharp pain caused by the pressure against one's underpants of a developing erection which necessitates the performance of an uphall (qv).

RADLETT (n.)
The single hemisphere of dried pea which is invariably found in an otherwise spotlessly clean saucepan.

RICHMOND (adj.)
Descriptive of the state that, very respectable elderly ladies get into if they have a little too much sherry, which, as everyone knows, does not make you drunk.

RICKLING (pt. vb.)
Fiddling around inside a magazine to remove all the stapled-in special offer cards that make it impossible to read.

ROSSETT (vb.)
To skulk in the cubicle of a public lavatory having done a particularly smelly poo until you can hear that everyone outside has left and won't wrinkle their noses at you when you come out.

SCRIBNER (n.)
One who sends holiday postcards to their local Chinese take-away.

SCUGOG (n.)
One whose mouth actually hangs open when watching something mildly interesting on the other side of the street.

SKIDDAW (vb.)
To break violently during a skipwith (qv), turn, and tunny-hop back upstairs when you realise that there is someone else in the house after all.

SKIPWITH (vb.)
To break off from a poo and bunny-hop downstairs with your pants round your ankles to answer the phone when you know there's no one else in the house.

SOMPTING (pt. vb.)
The practice of dribbling involuntarily into one's own pillow.

SOUTHWICK (n.)
A left-handed wanker.

SPRUCE KNOB (n.)
A genital aftershave which is supposed to be catching on in America.

SPURGER (n.)
One who in answer to the question "How are you?" actually tells you.

SQUIBNOCKET (n.)
That part of a car, the unexpected need for the replacement of which causes garage bills to be four times larger than the estimate.

STEENHUFFEL (n.)
One who is employed by a trade delegation or negotiating team to swell the numbers and make it look impressive when they walk out. There are currently 25,368 steenhuffels working at the UN in New York.

STELLING MINNIS (n.)
A traditional street dance. This lovely old gigue can be seen at any time of the year in the streets of the City of London or the courts of the Old Bailey. Wherever you see otherwise perfectly staid groups of bankers, barristers or ordinary members of the public moving along in a slightly syncopated walk, you may be sure that the stelling minnis is taking place. The phenomenon is caused by the fact that the dancers are trying not to step on the cracks in the pavement in case the bears get them.

STUTTGART (n.)
The aghast feeling one gets on returning from the bathroom to the bedroom to discover that the person one is about to sleep with looks hideously different without any clothes on.

SWEFLING (pt. vb.)
Using a special attachment to hoover a sofa.

TARVES (n.)
Pseudo-cairns. Small mounds of stones erected a few yards from mountain paths for the sole purpose of making you wonder why they're there.

TETNEY (adj.)
Not angry yet, but will be if one more thing goes wrong.

TWISP (n.)
The correct name for the little packet of salt in blue paper which Smiths can't decide whether or not to keep in their crisps.

UPHALL (vb.)
To adjust an erection through the trouser pocket so that it lies upwards, kept in place by the waistband of your pants. This eases the probus (qv).

WACCAMAW (n.)
An exotic Brazilian bird which makes its home in the audiences of BBC Light Entertainment Radio shows and screeches when it hears the word "bottom".

WARSLOW (n.)
Sequence of small casual gestures carefully planned to bring your watch surreptitiously into view. Much used during some of the longer string quartets of Bartok.

WAWNE (n.)
Badly suppressed yawn.

WINNIPEG (n.)
The stout wooden rod which film technicians insert into a horse to make it behave more impressively in the movies.

WINSTER (n.)
One who is mistakenly under the impression that they are charming.

YEBRA (n.)
A cross between a zebra and anything else which fancies zebras.

YEPES (n.)
A disease which will be discovered shortly that will make everyone wonder why on earth they got so upset about a little thing like AIDS.

YUKON (n.)
One who possesses an unseemly collection of Marmite.

Jesus' Birthday

It was Christmas day in the Christ family, and Jesus was in his usual mood. 'Why does my birthday have to fall on Christmas day,' he said crossly, as he did every year. 'I only get half the number of presents that everyone else gets. It's just not fair, just NOT FAIR.'

It wouldn't be long now till he started complaining about the fact that those few presents he did get were all hand-made by his father. He didn't like his father much. Sometimes he had these fantasies that his father wasn't his father at all, but that he was the illegitimate child of someone incredibly glamorous.

'Oh do stop complaining' said his mother, who was in the kitchen, doing the turkey. But, as ever, she was very mild about it. She felt so sorry for Jesus – he was such a lonely little boy, since all the children who should have been his friends had been slaughtered by Herod just after he was born.

'And can't you have a word with my godfathers,' said Jesus. 'Year after year it's the same old thing, two kinds of perfume and all that gold cutlery.'

Mary sighed. Jesus was right: it had been a real mistake appointing those three foreigners, but they were so well-dressed. Should have picked one

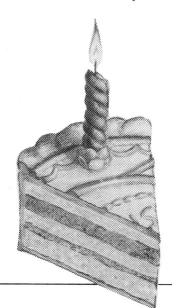

of those nice shepherds, she mused to herself. But not for long. In stormed Joseph.

'You going to have the dinner ready on time this year?' he asked rudely. Mary didn't bother to remind him that she had never once been late. Joseph had never trusted her since 7 months before Jesus was born and there was nothing she could do about it now.

Five minutes later they were sat around the table glumly.

'Say grace, darling, please,' said Mary.

'All right,' said Jesus. 'Our Father, Who art in heaven, hallowed be Thy name . . .'

'Do it properly,' said Joseph. Jesus had made up this little prayer, and was always trying to squeeze it in.

'All right. Dear God, two, four, six, eight, Bog in, don't wait.' They ate in silence.

Life is so boring, Jesus thought to himself. I hope things get a bit livelier when I grow up.

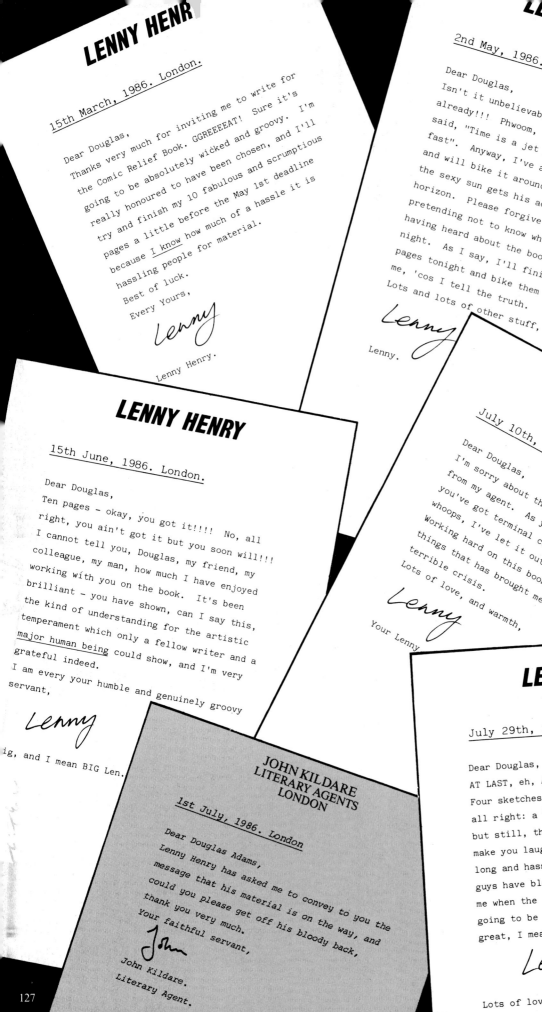

LENNY HENRY

15th March, 1986. London.

Dear Douglas,
Thanks very much for inviting me to write for the Comic Relief Book. GGREEEEAT! Sure it's going to be absolutely wicked and groovy. I'm really honoured to have been chosen, and I'll try and finish my 10 fabulous and scrumptious pages a little before the May 1st deadline because I know how much of a hassle it is hassling people for material.
Best of luck.
Every Yours,

Lenny

Lenny Henry.

LENNY HENRY

2nd May, 1986. London.

Dear Douglas,
Isn't it unbelievabubble how time flies. May already!!! Phwoom, whommm, whammy! As Dylan said, "Time is a jet plane, it moves too fast". Anyway, I've almost finished the stuff and will bike it around tomorrow as soon as the sexy sun gets his act together over the horizon. Please forgive me for that bit about pretending not to know who you were and never having heard about the book when you rang last night. As I say, I'll finish the 10 sex-hot pages tonight and bike them round. Believe me, 'cos I tell the truth.
Lots and lots of other stuff,

Lenny

Lenny.

LENNY HENRY

15th June, 1986. London.

Dear Douglas,
Ten pages - okay, you got it!!!! No, all right, you ain't got it but you soon will!!!! I cannot tell you, Douglas, my friend, my colleague, my man, how much I have enjoyed working with you on the book. It's been brilliant - you have shown, can I say this, the kind of understanding for the artistic temperament which only a fellow writer and a major human being could show, and I'm very grateful indeed.
I am every your humble and genuinely groovy servant,

Lenny

ig, and I mean BIG Len.

LENNY HENRY

July 10th, 1986. London.

Dear Douglas,
I'm sorry about that distinctly uncool letter from my agent. As you can imagine, life when you've got terminal cancer, isn't easy. O whoops, I've let it out. Still, don't worry. Working hard on this book is one of the few things that has brought me through this terrible crisis.
Lots of love, and warmth,

Lenny

Your Lenny

JOHN KILDARE
LITERARY AGENTS
LONDON

1st July, 1986. London

Dear Douglas Adams,
Lenny Henry has asked me to convey to you the message that his material is on the way, and could you please get off his bloody back, thank you very much.
Your faithful servant,

John

John Kildare.
Literary Agent.

LENNY HENRY

July 29th, 1986. London.

Dear Douglas,
AT LAST, eh, AT LAST!!!!! Here is the stuff. Four sketches and a short story! Hope they'r all right: a bit of a change of style for me but still, they make me laugh so I hope they make you laugh too. I'm sorry it has been s long and hassly, and just hope all the other guys have bloody well done their stuff. Tel me when the launch party is. I think it's going to be great, great book, and when I sa great, I mean, GGRERREEEAAAT!!!!!!!!! Wow!

Lenny

Lots of love, little Len, your baby.

Dear Douglas,

thanks very much for the <u>great</u> telegram, that arrived at 4 this morning. Sorry about not biking the stuff around last week. Truth is, it's got so difficult trying to work in London (traffic, telephones, you <u>know</u> that groove-less scene) that I've booked a cottage for a week in Wales, and will get it all done there. Sorry if it's a little late, but I hope it will be worth the waiting for. Fact of the matter is that I've had a POSITIVELY MIND-BENDING idea, and I suspect it may be a little more that just 10 little ole pages when it hotfoots your way at the end of the week. Can I just say, by the wayside, that I'm not at all annoyed by you nagging me and bugging me and leaving messages on my ansaphone all the time, I mean, five or six a day. I'm sure that's the way you <u>have</u> to behave in this kind of situation, and I'm really sorry that it makes you look like an utter berk.

Bad luck, stay cool,

Lenny

Lenny.

LENNY HENRY

<u>20th May, 1986. Wales.</u>

Dear Douglas,

It's done - FINISHED - COMPLETE!!! At last, eh!!!! Yes, at last I've finished the bit of work that has been stopping me doing your Comic Relief Book. I didn't want to tell you about it, brother, but I had this screenplay to finish and haven't till now been able to give the book a single moment's thought. Now, however, I'm cruising back from Dullsville, Wales and all the distractions of trying to live in a remote country cottage with no hot and cold running toilets, back to London where I can really move and groove. I'll bike the stuff round TOMORROW.

All my love, your little Lennikins.

Lenny

P.S. My wife Dawn also sends her love and says she wasn't annoyed by the phone always ringing and these telegrams arriving every hour either.

P.P.S. It was 3 pages wasn't it?

DOUGLAS ADAMS

<u>y 30th, 1986. London.</u>

ear Lenny,

hank you for your excellent contribution. If our book can be anything like as good as the Monty Python Big Red Book from which your four sketches were so carefully cut, it will indeed be a great book. As for the short story - I think it is one of P.G. Wodehouse's best.

Douglas

Love Douglas.

LENNY HENRY

<u>August 15th, 1986. London</u>

Dear Douglas,

I've got to be honest with you. The truth of the matter is that I've been having a terrible, terrible time in my marriage to Dawn and I have definitely split up, once and for all. It's been hard, and one of the few things that has pulled me through is your patience and kindness about this book, which I must unfortunately now inform you I will not be contributing to.

Lenny

Love Lenny (Henry).

December 15th 1986

Dear Douglas,
Look, if you really want something for your bloody book, why not just use all those letters, fix the spelling, that sort of thing, should be fab. It's really amazing here in Jamaica. Hope the book goes FANTASTICALLY well. Tell me when the launch party is and Merry Christmas!!! Love Dawn and Lenny.

COMIC RELIEF LIVE

On April 4, 5 and 6 a delightful get-together was held in the foyer of London's historic Shaftesbury Theatre, home of The Theatre of Comedy. There was much drink and gaiety and, for those who tired of the company, a little cabaret was staged next door in the main auditorium. Couldn't drag myself away from the wit of Lord Busby Berkeley and his delightful wife Melons, but those who did said there were many whacky, zany and mad-cap moments, as the photos bear witness.

Pamela Auctions off Eric Clapton's Instrument.

Rowan Atkinson Breaks Wind Discreetly.

So Does Rik Mayall.

Three of the Young Ones Share a Joke Together.

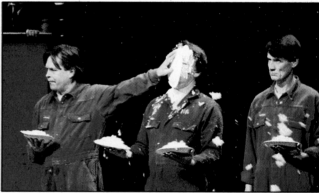
Terry Gilliam Illustrates American Table Manners.

Billy Connolly Dies on Stage.

Rowan Does Something That Makes Kate Very Happy.

Rabbi Glitter Prepares for Circumcision Rites.

Rory Bremner Does an Unsuccessful Imitation of Samantha Fox.

Nancy Gives Ronnie Comic Relief.

Lenny Henry Gives Comic Relief to the Invisible Man.

Dawn French & Jennifer Saunders Wait Outside Prince Andrew's Bedroom.

Vyv Welcomes the Photographer to the Party.

Frank Bruno Dressed to Take on Thatcher.

Invisible Man Brings his Family Along to Join in the Fun.

Rik Graphically Demonstrates the Number of Gospels.

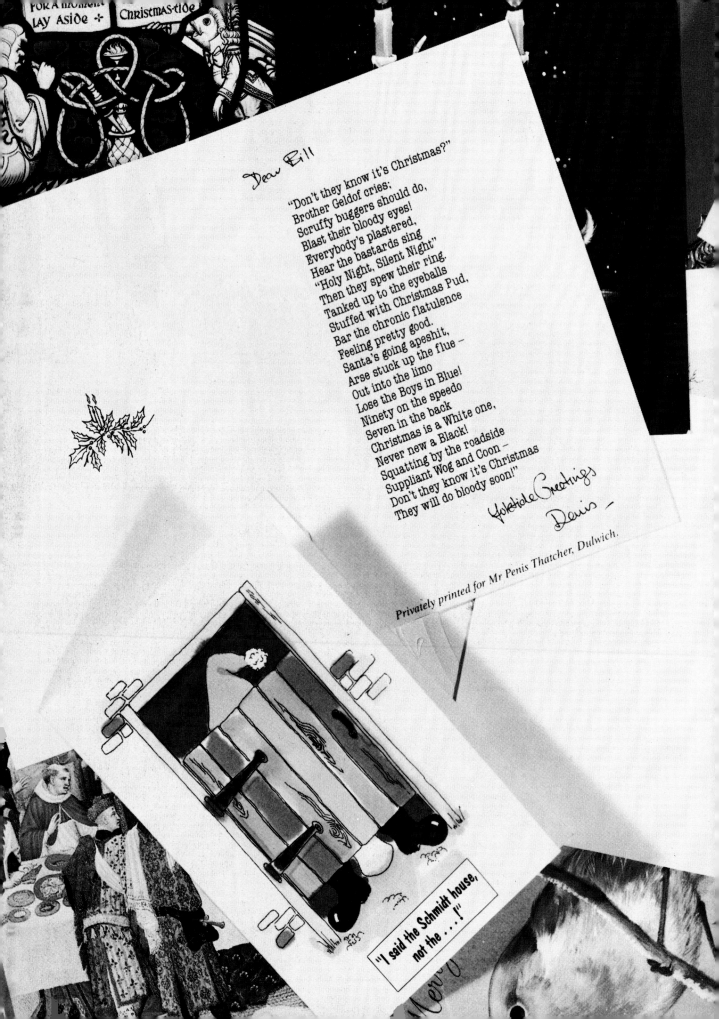

Dear Bill

"Don't they know it's Christmas?"
Brother Geldof cries;
Scruffy buggers should do,
Blast their bloody eyes!
Everybody's plastered,
Hear the bastards sing
"Holy Night, Silent Night"
Then they spew their ring.
Tanked up to the eyeballs
Stuffed with Christmas Pud,
Bar the chronic flatulence
Feeling pretty good.
Santa's going apeshit,
Arse stuck up the flue –
Out into the limo
Lose the Boys in Blue!
Ninety on the speedo
Seven in the back
Christmas is a White one,
Never new a Black!
Squatting by the roadside
Suppliant Wog and Coon –
Don't they know it's Christmas
They will do bloody soon!"

Yuletide Greetings
Denis –

Privately printed for Mr Penis Thatcher, Dulwich.

"I said the Schmitt house,
not the . . . !"

Hoppo, you old sod! Where's the bottle of Old Gran Grauddad you promised me over the Libyan shindig? I thought the idea was to put a stop to terrorism, not tourism. Minds gene I imagine.

Affectionate Christmas Greetings

here to the emancipated spouse

Yrs aye

Denis

Denis & Margaret Thatcher
10 Downing Street
London SW1

To His Royal Highness Philip Duke of Edinburgh

Hope you like this snap of Mother Christmas distributing the goodies: I picked it up some years ago in Gay Paree

DENIS AND MARGARET THATCHER

GIVING

can

CHRISTMAS COMES ROUND ONCE A YEAR

D.T. some days later

Yrs aye

Denis

P.S. Wot a word to Betty

Editions Naughty Postcards, Rue de Pic, Paris 69

...en on the desperately rich"

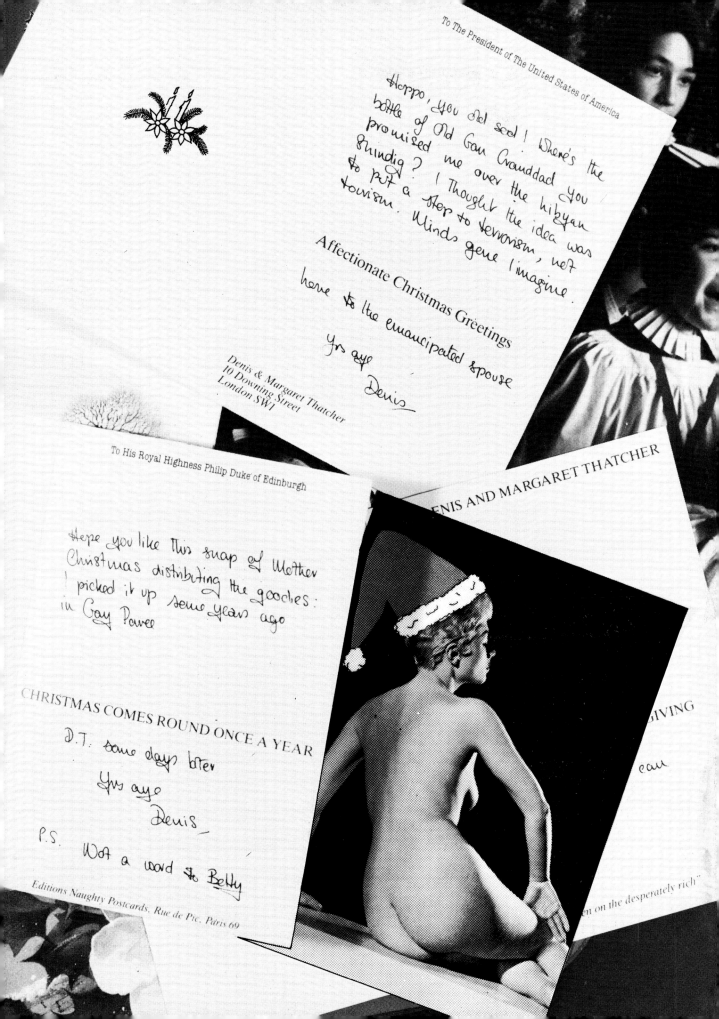

The Official Supplement to The Official Supplement to The Meaning of Liff

Since compiling The Official Supplement to the Meaning of Liff
it has become clear that some serious omissions were omitted from it,
so here they aren't.

Duglas Adams

Alresford
Noise made by a ploughman eating a ploughman's lunch.

Wolverton
Noise made by a ploughman eating another
ploughman's ploughman's lunch.

Horsham
Exclamation made by other ploughman on turning
back to discover that his lunch has been wolvertoned.

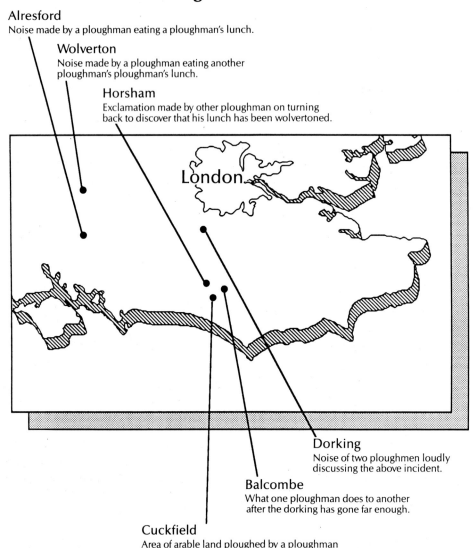

Dorking
Noise of two ploughmen loudly
discussing the above incident.

Balcombe
What one ploughman does to another
after the dorking has gone far enough.

Cuckfield
Area of arable land ploughed by a ploughman
who has recently been dorked to and balcombed.

The Official Supplement to The Official Supplement to The Official Supplement to The Meaning of Liff

Sorry, we seem to have omitted an "o".
Here it is.

O

Enjoy.

Continued from page 31
nevertheless plenty of writhing limbs and heaving bodies, eyes glazed over with a frenzied lust reducing all present to nothing more than desires, and pulsing blood, and hungry, searching mouths, all of which added up to a very special edition of *Gardeners' Question Time*.

ANSWERS TO QUIZ ON PAGE 27

1. Wet palms
2. Derek Nimmo. The others are all Turkish.
3. Black Rod. (score half a point for Sheffield Wednesday).
4. Under a table at Lee Ho Fuk's.
5. Cannabis resin rolled in pink silk chiffon.
6. Jeffrey Archer. The others are all politicians.
7. They are the four dirtiest words in the English language.
8. (a) 127 inches (not verified)
   (b) Mike Gatting
   (c) i. Boasting
       ii. baby powder.
9. Jeffrey Archer. The others are all novelists.

Continued from page 42
stuff and wrap carefully in silver foil, then coat with the marmalade and Bovril mixture. Pour the warm gin over the cold chopped fried egg and leave to stand for one hour, then combine with the Vim and minced crumpet before folding in the mixture together and serving *immediately* on a bed of sorrel and rabbits' fur. To accompany this unusual and delicious dish we would suggest our own special cocktail:

HORSE'S TESTICLES
1 measure Guinness
1 measure Blue Bols
1 whole chicken skin
2 large knobs of lard.
Allow the chicken skin to stand in cold water overnight,
(Cont. p.95 . . .)

Continued from page 66
severed from her shoulders and the pipes and arteries sticking out obscenely and spouting blood in great gouts, astonishingly crimson. "Geoffrey," I said sternly, "you're not in Solihull now," before turning away and walking, slowly but forever, out of his life.

Continued from page 13
since Friday, so you can see why I am a little concerned. Concerned, Hornchurch, Essex.

Dear Concerned,

Yes, and I think you have every right to be concerned. You've obviously made every reasonable effort you can from your side, and I think what you have to do now is to get out of the house at once, burn it down if necessary, and then notify the police immediately unless you think you can get out of the country via one of the channel ports before nightfall. Let me stress that there is nothing for you to feel at all guilty about, it's just one of those things. I come across similar cases very often in my line of work, and I do assure you that it is not a goat.
Marge.

Continued from page 17
and also eaten it, but he later denied the charges. Nevertheless he remains the first member of the House of Lords to be prosecuted under the 1827 Sexual Offences (Agricultural Machinery) Act.

Continued from page 81
simple method is absolutely infallible, and if you don't believe us, try it yourself. Our guinea-pig, Dennis, a 26-year-old creative director with DBWCS, tried it for a week, during which time
* A TRAFFIC WARDEN apologised and tore up the ticket
* His TAX INSPECTOR resigned — but not before paying him a rebate of ALL THE TAX he had paid SINCE 1981
* His DOCTOR rang up and said he didn't have AIDS after all.
* He went to bed with NINETEEN WOMEN, none of whom he had known more than half an hour.
* He BOUGHT four cases of the Beychevelle '76 at an AVERAGE PRICE OF £1.26 a bottle.
Now you know the secret! Go out and try it for yourself!

Continued from page 53
which *still contained traces of human head."*
The pause which followed was broken by a choked cry from Mr Moore.
"Yes. Mr Moore," said Poirot. "Our should I say . . . Obergruppenführer Waldheim?"
"No," said Mr Moore.
"I thought not," said the detective, grimly. "You see, the truth is . . . I do not know who did this thing. Even I am baffled. But . . ."
"Yes?" whispered Miss Moncrieff, eagerly.
". . . I can't say I really give a fuck," said Poirot, smiling.

SHAKESPEARE & COMIC RELIEF
A MODEL ESSAY FOR 'O' & 'A' LEVEL ENGLISH CANDIDATES
Learn this essay and reproduce. Guaranteed Grade A standard!

Q: What, in the context of Shakespearean tragedy, is Comic Relief?

A: Shakespeare, in his great tragedies, *Hamlet, King Lear, Antony & Cleopatra, Othello, Brindius — Duke of Corinth, Julius Ceasar* and *Macbeth* made extensive use of the technique we now know as Comic Relief: the suspension and heightening of tragic action by the intervention of broad comedy.

There are many explanations for this. Some critics think it was done to keep the lower-class, less educated members of the audience (the 'groundlings' as they were called) entertained, others believe it was a deliberate dramatic strategy designed to show farce in grotesque contrast with tragedy. Other critics argue that those critics are talking out of their fat, Oxbridge arses and should get down on to the frigging streets and see what's going on out there.

It is this panoply of critical choices that makes Shakespearean scholarship the thrilling pursuit it is. It is my view that such extremes of viewpoint only prove the rich complexity of the works of Shakespeare, the Swan of Avon, the Warwickshire minstrel who wins our hearts and minds in his exciting plays and poems — even if the poems are sometimes frankly gay. (Not that there's anything wrong with that, for goodness sake. A young sunny lad in tights and ruff is a fruit in the garden of love that few can ever resist plucking. If William, our First of Poets, Chief Singer of the Human Heart, the greatest Englishmen that ever drew breath, liked a drive up Chocolate Lane now and again, who are we to complain?)

However, back to the subject — Comic Relief. In arguably his greatest tragic work, *Brindius – Duke of Cornith,* Shakespeare raises the art of Comic Relief to new heights. Brindius, having mistakenly blinded and then decapitated Bottia, his wife, in mistake for Cranno her lover, is brought the news of what he has done by Mellow, his clown. Brindius is horror-struck.

> *Thus do the gods make habcocks of us all*
> *Issuing our own reeking deeds back upon*
> *The proper hazard of our gain. My duchess!*
> *Even the very spike of my intent is botched*
> *Upon the main, to plague the husband in's kind.*
> *My duchess! Now do we see how Nature grosses*
> *E'en the weed and rank of purpose. My duchess!*

This, for Brindius, is the turning point. Here his sanity collapses. His reason is built upon the natural order of things, a natural order which his dreadful murder has overturned. It will be the function of the tragedy now to re-establish that order. However, at this critical point, when Brindius is covered in the blood of his beloved wife, instead of taking the traditional, serious route, Shakespeare startlingly opts to go for the gag. Mellow the Clown interrupts the action with this extraordinary speech:

> *Shall not your servant send for Cranno that he might do aught to prick her awake? For it's a yard to a Bedford cockerel that his pricks are good for rousing a chick of a morn. When that good cock rises and crows, why, my lord, might not all wake?*

BRINDIUS   *Peace, fool!*

MELLOW   *Aye, my lord. Piece indeed — such a piece, an it please you — as might (in the breadth of it, and sure in the height of it, an I doubt not in the length of it) pierce the peace of the morning and frolic the lass awake to cry "Come! Good morning, Come!" and so give Cranno the horn and then should your mourning cease, indeed.*

The substance of Mellow's speech is this: "You are mourning your wife's death and trying to wake her with your speeches. Shall I not rather send for Cranno, her lover, whom you meant to kill instead of her? Roosters are the traditional way of waking people up and Cranno is known to have an enormous cock. Let Cranno arouse her with a good rogering and your mourning will cease. How about it, matey?"

Nothing could be more startling or tactless, you say. But, no, Shakespeare knows better. Look what this complex image cluster of wordplay and tactless filth has achieved.

1) It intensifies the agony of Brindius, providing a painful human moment.

2) It stops Brindius from transforming himself, through language, from jealous, diseased murderer into passionate, tragic hero. He has not yet earned the right to versify himself into the Valhalla of poetic heroes and Mellow anchors him to the real, earthy world.

3) But finally, and most importantly, it gives the audience, who are bored stiff with all this grim stuff about people killing each other in the most massively unlikely situations, a chance to have a really good dirty laugh before they get back to the boring bit about the gods, the wheel of fire etc. etc. etc. Let's face facts, half of Shakespeare's plays are a load of old rot, and the only reason we read them is because the poor bugger was gay as a coot, and not to read them, but rather to read the plays of a redblooded hetero like Harold Pinter, would be discriminating against gays.

And so we see how Shakespeare uses Comic Relief both to throw tragedy into relief and to relieve the audience from tragedy with cunning allusions to the enormous todgers that were the joy of his private life.

Crudeword Crossword Cracked

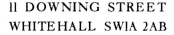
11 DOWNING STREET
WHITEHALL SW1A 2AB

Thank You
Live Aid
and Comic Relief

From those it benefited.

We'd just like to say a very big thank you to everyone who gave up their time and energy to make it all possible, and particularly to the people who made contributions, most particularly those who bought the records.

We can only say we were very grateful indeed for the money, and would like to urge you to keep it up. So, once again, thanks for the VAT.

Yours truly,

Nigel Lawson

Nigel Lawson.

P.S. Do you think you could possibly make the book more than half full of pictures? That way we can slap some VAT on that as well and make sure all the money doesn't go to those bloody Africans.

COMIC RELIEF

In 1985 a group of comedians, comic writers, producers and many others decided to use their talents to raise money for the crisis in Africa under the title COMIC RELIEF. These people have so far raised half a million pounds through the re-release of 'Living Doll' sung by Cliff Richard and the Young Ones; three COMIC RELIEF live shows which were shown on BBC Television; and an album of the shows.

In Africa, COMIC RELIEF continues to give money to SAVE THE CHILDREN FUND and OX-FAM. We have bought seed in Ethiopia, supported workshops which maintain the fleets of trucks and Land Rovers in Sudan and Ethiopia and have also funded the doctors and nurses and bought medical supplies for a large refugee camp. In the future, COMIC RELIEF will be working with S.C.F. and OXFAM to establish long-term projects for child care, water and agriculture which will initiate the recovery of famine-hit communities and work towards giving them an element of security for the future. COMIC RELIEF is thinking about that future NOW.

On the home front we have given 20% of money raised to CHARITY PROJECTS who have made a series of grants to small groups and organisations working with young people facing the problems of homelessness, drug abuse and disability. CHARITY PROJECTS singles out small projects which often do not have the means to draw on large donors and makes grants in response to specific requests.

All the material in this book was specially written and donated by its contributors, and the publishers are giving all their profits to COMIC RELIEF.

Thank you for buying this book.

If you are concerned that Parliament should reflect your continued concern about hunger in Africa cut out the drawing by Ron Cobb opposite and post it to the House of Commons. Please tell your M.P. that you care.
You can also send to Oxfam for details of their Hungry for Change campaign.
Oxfam, Oxfam House, 274 Banbury Road, Oxford OX2 7DZ

C

_____

_____

_____

Your Address

_____

Your Name

Fold B ▬ ▬ ▬ ▬ ▬ ▬ ▬ ▬ ▬ ▬ ▬ ▬ ▬ ▬ ▬ ▬ ▬

**HOUSE OF COMMONS
LONDON SW1A 0AA**

Fold A ▬ ▬ ▬ ▬ ▬ ▬ ▬ ▬ ▬ ▬ ▬ ▬ ▬ ▬ ▬ ▬ ▬

Enter your M.P.'s name and your message.
Fold along line A and line B and tape along C.
Affix postage-stamp and *post*.